True Crime Story
I Survived A Monster

Opal Roux

DEDICATION

For the girls.

CONTENTS

ACKNOWLEDGMENTS

A big thank you to the following people for their in depth interviews for this book. Thank you to Paul Wells, best friend of victim, Amy Alden; Mark Foster, son of victim, Floyd Foster; John Pyskaty, skiing and hunting buddy of Ralph and Betty Lee's big sister, Gail Hanson Kent.

Thank you to my good friend and editor, Cathy McElhaney and to Genevieve Rose for bringing Betty Lee and I together to write this book. Thank you for your friendship and support throughout the years, Cathy. Because of you, this book sees the light of day and Betty Lee finally gets to tell her story.

Thank you to my loving Aunt Judy for her undying support throughout the years. She once sold my very first book in her shop and often calls to ask about my latest release and to congratulate me. Her support has meant the world to me and she will always be my very special, favorite aunt who I adore. I love you, Aunt Judy.

Thank you to my husband, Michael for your support and advice while writing this very disturbing book. Thank you for encouraging me to finish it and most of all for your love and belief in me. You are my rock.

FORWARD BY THE AUTHOR

Back in 2011 when Betty Lee first contacted me about writing this book, I listened to her tell her story in gut wrenching detail, blown away by the evil she had experienced as a 15-year-old girl. Not only had she just spent her first Christmas without her beloved father but she was faced with fighting off one of the biggest sexual predators of the century. If you talk to Betty Lee, she can take you back to that fateful Christmas night of 1973 in the blink of an eye. I was only three-years-old; playing with the new toy kitchen my folks had given me for Christmas while Betty Lee was fighting for her life.

    A handful of authors have attempted to write this book before but all of them backed out, not feeling the project was right for them or other work duties getting in the way. I am the only female to attempt to write this book and Betty Lee now feels that my gender was the key to writing it. She told me a woman needs to write this book because only a woman knows what it feels like to be overpowered by a man, unable to escape for the simple fact that a man is physically stronger than a woman.

    To escape a killer like her monster, a lot has to happen. The urge to survive has to be stronger than anything that person has ever faced. Luck. You have to be lucky enough to be in a location with other human beings close enough to help you. God. There's no doubt about it. Without God, she wouldn't be here today.

She carries a lot of guilt for surviving while other girls did not but with that guilt comes a burning duty to tell this story.

She wanted this book written for the girls. The authorities know of six people Ralph Raymond Andrews killed but while in prison, he confessed to raping, eviscerating, slaughtering and killing 40 more girls. Only God and Ralph know the true body count. This is the story of the modern day Jack-the-Ripper. He killed for a period of three decades; from the 70's through the 90's, throughout Illinois, Wisconsin and Michigan. And he was a coward to the end, dying in prison in 2006, too afraid to undergo life-saving heart surgery. I find it ironic that a monster who took such pride in cutting up his victims was too afraid of a doctor with a scalpel.

This book was not an easy book to write and my first non-fiction book. I typically write romance novels and children's books. My editor heard about the story and thought I might be interested in writing the book. And she was right. Sometimes the ugly realities of life and death should be exposed. People have suffered greatly. Many girls have died because this man was born.

Thank you, Betty Lee for trusting me to write your story. I wish to God you'd never crossed paths with Ralph. ~ Opal Roux

1 THE NIGHT OF THE ATTACK

December 25, 1973 ~ Evanston, Illinois

I was fifteen-years-old. Christmas was hard that year with my dad gone. My mother was suicidal and wanted nothing more than to lie down and die. All the life insurance money from my dad's death was gone and we were about to lose our house. It was up to me to keep things together. I had to get a tree for my brother and make dinner.

My life had steamrolled into a world that was pretty bizarre. Everything seemed and felt unreal. Maybe I was still in shock from my dad's death. I don't know.

I do know that I felt invincible back in 1973. I remember that Christmas evening like it was last night. Pam and I were best friends; a beautiful freckle-faced brunette, brown-eyed girl with a good figure. She lived in an enormous mansion. It blew my mind that she had an entire wing of her own at her parents' house.

Kinda nice for a teenager.

Her step-father owned the mortuary where my dad's funeral service was held. Talk about a small world. And I was constantly reminded of my father's death just because she was my best friend. All the dead people in town paid for her house. Talk about creepy. That was my life. Death seemed to smother me, always whispering in my ear. I was pretty familiar with the dark, morbid side of life many teenagers weren't accustomed to.

Gorgeous Pam showed up at my house on Christmas evening in sexy black jeans and an off white fox fur coat. Even though I couldn't get away from death, I could go with the mortician's kid and forget about it and try to be a teenager for one night. A blizzard was blowing and I welcomed the cold. The sting on my face helped me forget my pain.

I still remember what I wore that night. I walked the snowy streets in flared blue jeans with fur and a blue jean jacket with peacock feathers and beadwork. I had sewn it myself and it looked pretty hot. The bell bottoms went right over my platforms to the ground. My coat was from my cousin's grandmother from Germany. A black seal fur coat. I loved it. I wore a black silk t-shirt that a friend loaned to me. He told me that if anything happened to it, he'd kill me. He never got that t-shirt back. It was cut off of me a few hours later.

Back then everyone hitchhiked, especially in a blizzard. We hitched a ride to this one guy's house in Evanston. I don't even remember exactly how long it took or how we got there. On a wing and a prayer I guess. But that was normal for my life at the time. We were on Main Street and Chicago Avenue. There was a little house in the alley by the L train tracks. When we got to the party there was nothing going on.

Totally dead.

We had a few sips of beer and maybe a joint and then decided to blow that place. Way too boring for a Christmas night and not enough action to keep my mind off my sorrows. We had to climb the fire stairs in the back of the alley when we decided to go see this guy named Tony.

That one fateful decision has haunted me all my life.

We were freezing and could easily hitch a ride to his place, so we did. Within minutes, a two-door opal paneled station wagon pulled up. The windows were totally fogged up. Pam hopped in the back as he held the driver's side door open for us and I scooted in, anxious to be near the car's heater. The guy was taller than me but just a little bit. He looked to be about five foot nine and I thought for sure he was O.C.D. just by the way he combed his hair or I would have thought that if the term were used back in '73. When I think back on it, that's what hits me.

Perfect hair.

Like a scientist. Where was his pocket protector? This guy looked like he'd make an A in Chemistry. The kind of guy you'd hire to organize your bills while doing a science project. Nerdy and smart, like a brainy accountant. And on the wimpy side too. Definitely not boyfriend material. I was sure we were safe with this dork. He looked like he was absent when God was giving out testosterone injections.

But I had it all wrong. Terribly wrong.

Ralph Raymond Andrews.

The most evil man I will ever meet.

I had some shitty luck after all I'd been through. My mom wanted to die and we were close to losing our house after my dad died. I was surprised

I had held it together for as long as I did. Meeting this monster was like the triple hex from Hell. When they say it can't get worse, don't believe them. It can always get worse. And it did. Every minute that ticked by proved to me that my life just a few minutes before, back on that snowy street wasn't so bad after all.

Ralph decided that night he was going to kill us when he picked us up hitchhiking. I knew we were in big trouble when I saw there were no door handles. All I could see were the inside workings of the car door.

"What happened to the door?" I asked.

"This car was on fire. It was burnt out," he responded.

Our fate was sealed the second we got in the car. We had no way out but through him. My heart dropped. I chill shot through me. We were in big trouble. In two seconds flat, this guy went from harmless dork to total freak and I could feel his evil. Like a dog smells a rat in a hole. My hopes soared when I saw my friend, Chris at a gas station. I told Ralph to roll down the window. I was surprised he did as I asked. My heart sped up.

"Hey, Chris. You want to go to Tony's?"

"No, man. I'm just filling up my car so it doesn't freeze. I'm getting out of this shit," Chris called back through the blowing storm.

Ralph drove on when the light turned green.

"You can just let us out up a ways," I said, trying my best not to sound frightened.

Just like he was talking about how to make a sandwich, he told me what he wanted instead. "I like to see what pretty little girls look like with their clothes off."

"Look, just let us go and I'll forget this ever happened," I said.

"That ain't gonna happen," he responded with an even, calm voice.

Pam leaned over the back seat and, grabbed him around the throat and tried to choke him. It was like instinct for Ralph. He didn't flinch, pause or even look at her when he grabbed a hidden knife, threw his hand back and stabbed her in the lung. Blood spurted everywhere like a thumb over a hose. I glanced back as blood squirted, hitting the car ceiling, the windows, the seats, my face. She went into catatonic shock. Her world had come crashing down in an instant. Nothing violent had ever happened in her innocent, rich girl's life. She thought she was street smart. We all did. She was like a porcelain doll. This guy had stabbed my very best friend. My mind was scrambling, reaching for a solution out of this hell. I wasn't going down without a fight. I would survive this demon.

I caught sight of a box of Kleenex on the floor and I calmly told Pam's killer that I had to help stop the bleeding. She wouldn't look me in the eye when I turned and spoke to her. I told her to press down so she wouldn't bleed to death.

And then I turned to face this monster who had us trapped in a bloody car with no way out. When I looked into his eyes, my soul deflated.

I knew we were going to die. There was

nothing in his eyes. He was positively terrifying. In the blink of an eye, he had switched gears, like a master of disguise. He'd been as harmless as a dorky bookkeeper.

And now he was the best kind of predator, like an African lion.

And we were the prey.

But I was going to be that one percent. The one little bunny
that got away.

I was going to fight harder than I'd ever fought for anything in all my life.
He had the knife against my throat while we were driving.

My mind was whirring, going through a list of options, deciding my next move. By now the whole car is like a bloody massacre, filled with Pam's blood, splattered all over the place. I couldn't even remember what color the interior was. It was all red. He pressed the knife to my throat as he plowed through the slick, wintry streets while the snow's blowing like there's no tomorrow. And I wasn't sure if there was or not.

The thought floored me.

The three of us were all panting; him with excitement, Pam with terror and I was frantic, wracking my brain, trying to figure out how the fuck I'd get out of that car alive. I asked him if I could turn on the radio. I don't remember why. Maybe to distract him, maybe to give myself more time to think. He didn't answer.

"Please, we need to take Pam to the

hospital," I pleaded.

He didn't respond as he entered Eden Expressway toward Wisconsin when I knew the hospital was past the lake in the other direction.

I said, "Hey, if you just let us off at a hospital, we won't say a thing."

He said, "You already know my name."

A cop pulled up to us. I looked over and Ralph said, "If you even think of it, I'll slit your throat and he'll never see you. Do you understand me, little girl?"

And I did. I knew he was serious. I wanted to cry. He continued going 50 to 60 mph and told me in gory details about Amy Alden and other girls, how they were shot and eviscerated. My ears were assaulted, like a terrible whistle was screeching in my ear as he spoke. Every word was a new word of unspeakable horror.

He told me he was taking us to Skokie Lagoons where he would tie me up while he would torture and murder Pam. He said he'd peel her with a knife like a fucking vegetable because that was the best way to have sex because when the body is in its death throes, it clenches and that was the only way he could cum.

"Why did you kill them?" I asked.

"Because they smelled like pot," he said.

"Good. Do you mind if I smoke then?"

He let me and I started to think, knowing the cannabis would help calm my mind, separate my senses. Balance me. He was talking about how many people he killed. It hit me that he's completely insane, just talking as if he's shooting the shit when there's blood everywhere. I'd never seen so much blood. It just blew my mind. I had no idea how Pam was still alive or how much longer she had to live.

The marijuana steadied me, calmed me a bit. I was thinking, looking around, scanning the floor boards, everything in the car.

"Open your coat," he ordered.

And in a flash, he stuck his hand violently down my shirt. His murdering hands were all over my breasts. I felt myself unraveling. I knew I'd soon snap. And I willed myself to stay there, to not become the zombie Pam was in the back seat and just accept this fate. I was thinking, Oh my God, how dare you do this to me. I've been raped before.

Pam was still in the backseat, frozen solid, just lying there. I knew she would be no help and I decided right then and there that if I was going to die, he had to die with me. I knew I had to get past him to get out of that bloody car and if he drove to the lagoons, I knew we wouldn't have a chance. He would stab me just like Pam. What in the hell was I going to do? How was I going to get out of this? I refused to be raped and killed.

When he pulled down my pants, I heard a voice inside my head and I swear to God it was my father. He said, "Turn the wheel all the way around!"

It was an order, not a request. The sound of my dead father's voice in my head echoed so loud that it forced me to grab the steering wheel and I turned it all the way around, as fast as I could. I twirled it, yanking it around with my left arm. I put it into a gridlock so that it slid sideways. The tires hit a patch of ice and barreled down into a fifteen foot embankment.

When the car came to a crashing halt, he whipped his head around and stared at me. I'd never seen another human being so enraged. I had one pissed off serial killer on my hands. If he wanted to kill me before, he wanted to tear me to pieces now.

"What did you do, you filthy bitch?"

I screamed at him inside my head. *You aren't getting away this time, mother fucker!*

I grabbed his crotch, wanting to twist his balls off. I wanted to throw all that evil back onto him. So I did.

"Fuck a corpse," I replied, staring back.

Problem was, the fucker enjoyed me fighting back. We eyed each other like circling wolves and then we both went at one another, grunting and wrestling like hell for the knife. Somehow I managed to push the knife into him twice.

This knife was so unbelievably sharp, like he took it to a stone forever. I truly believe my father helped me push it in, along with a fleet of angels who surrounded me at that crucial moment in time.

I stabbed him twice and he didn't feel it, didn't flinch for one second. I was trying with both arms on one of his to try to keep it from jabbing me. I don't know how long this took but I think he punched me and my head just cracked and I fought through it.

My legs were pinned and my back was to the door. I managed to pull both of my feet up and kicked him in the balls. He came back stronger, punched me in the face again, on top of me with both knees, blowing his rotten breath all over me.

"For the love of God, Pam! Help me!"

Pam didn't move and I said, fuck it, I couldn't hold on and I let go. The knife slid inside me.

So fast.

He called me a filthy fucking bitch and the spray of blood-oh my God-it went everywhere! He licked his lips and smiled at me. Blood gushed from my wound like a broken fire hydrant. I'm sure that from outside onlookers the car resembled a snow globe of blood.

From out of nowhere a car horn blared.

Hope trickled into me.

Fear soon replaced that tiny grain of hope. Every time I took a breath, blood flowed from my mouth. I was afraid he'd stab me again.

The car horn sounded once more. "Does anyone need help down there?"

And the composure that came over him was unbelievable. He unrolled the window and peeked outside.

"I'm a doctor," Ralph called out.

"He murdered us!" I yelled.

I knew he was thinking of what to do. I had caught him off guard for half a second so I kicked him as hard as I could with my platforms. He flew out of the car.

The man outside yelled at him. "Get the fuck out of the car!"

I had stuck my thumb in my chest to make it stop. I don't know how I knew to do that. Survival instinct I guess. I reached for Pam by flipping the seat with a button. When I pulled on her, blood spurted everywhere but she managed to follow me out. I couldn't believe she was still conscious. As soon as we reached the top of the embankment, she yelled, "You murdered my best friend!"

And I thought, *Now she fucking talks!* Then I passed out cold.

The next thing I remember is riding in the man's car to the hospital.

It kissed my heart but also punctured my left lung. I'd been transported to Highland Park Hospital and I was bleeding out fast. The paramedics dumped bag after bag of blood into me and ran out on the way because I have rare AB RH negative blood.

2 FOR THE GIRLS

And this is just the beginning of the story. I believe Ralph Raymond Andrews is the biggest serial killer in the history of the United States. But time and time again, he wiggled out of trouble. There was never enough evidence and he was very convincing as the wimpy weakling who'd been attacked by some crazy kids wanting to hitch a ride, buy marijuana or rob him. Even when you look at an old photograph of him, you'll never understand how convincing he was, how very skilled he was at playing the part of the helpless, ultra conservative man who'd never harm a fly.

And because of that, even when he was a major suspect of his many crimes, he was considered "not dangerous" and often obtained a work release until the trial, which won him more time to drive the city bus and find his next victim.

I had to write this book. Not just to tell my story but for all the girls. For all the girls who don't have a voice now. For the unsolved deaths. The girls who are still missing, beneath the cold earth, long ago decayed and gone but not forgotten. They had mothers and father, sisters and brothers, grandparents, school friends and teachers who cared about them and they never got a chance to live. Never got a chance to finish high school, go to prom, get married, make love for the first time, have babies of their own and grandchildren to bake cookies for and take to the zoo. Their lives were snuffed out in the most terrifying way, at the hands of what I call the Devil's Disciple. And to think I know how helpless each one of those girls felt, knowing they would soon die.

Remembering the terror, the absolute horror, trying my damnedest to fight off this monster. It rips out my soul to know that those girls were forced to give up for the simple reason that they were too physically weak. They had no choice. There wasn't enough adrenaline in their veins or they didn't have a weapon like I did.

My platform boots.

Or it just wasn't their day. It was their day to die. Their day to say goodbye to the world. To close their eyes and watch the light fade into black as a knife slid into their heart like it did mine. They gasped their last breaths as he tortured them, tears falling down their faces as they thought of what in the hell their mothers and fathers would do without them. As they realized all they'd lost and that God wasn't coming to save them. They'd get to God but he wasn't coming. They weren't ready to see their maker. They had their youth, years and years to live but too bad for them. Life isn't fair. And sometimes it's so hideously evil, I can't even begin to make sense of the horror.

Shit luck landed them on Ralph's bus from Hell, giving him easy access to a herd of girls who just might trust him enough to take a ride home from him as they walked from the bus stop to home a few blocks away after he parked the bus. He'd stop his opal station wagon and smile, wearing his little scientist eye glasses, his hair perfectly parted and combed over, not a strand out of place.

That easy smile.

He was the bus driver for God's sake. Kids saw him every day. He opened those big bus doors and we all climbed on, waving at him, totally trusting this man to take us home.

He took enough of us home, that's for sure.

All the way home.

To a final resting place.

But he didn't take me home and he never will. After I recovered in the hospital, I wanted nothing more than to end his life. Little did I know that he would consume my life for eons. I would testify at countless trials, talk to grieving mothers and fathers, friends of the victims and bond with them like family because I had survived and I knew what their girls had endured.

The guilt I felt for surviving ate at me with each new trial, with every tear shed for every girl who suffered and died at his hands. I felt a huge responsibility to help put him away but it was decades until I got my wish, after he squirmed and slithered his way out of every conviction like a snake born in deepest, darkest Hell.

Not only did I testify at many trials, I had to stand strong against the accusations that I attacked and robbed Ralph Andrews on that fateful Christmas night. I thought life couldn't get worse but I was wrong. My mother believed me to be guilty of robbing Ralph and thought I brought all this upon myself.

Sure, I was a wild kid. I was 15-years-old and deeply depressed after my father's death. I wanted to get away, party with my best girlfriend and cut loose. I wanted to numb my mind, forget that my dad was dead. I was Daddy's girl, smothered with affection from my adoring father. A thick blanket of death engulfed my world when I'd lost him and all I wanted to do was forget the pain, forget that I had to plaster on a fake smile for Christmas and get the tree myself because my mother just couldn't deal with it. I had to grow up overnight and be a mom to my mentally challenged brother and I felt like a kid myself.

A HAPPY CHRISTMAS IN THE 60's. (From top to
bottom. Sister Gail, Brother Billy, Mother Dorothy,
Father William and Betty Lee as a child.)

(From Left to Right, Top to Bottom; Sister Gail, Father William, Betty Lee, Mother Dorothy, Brother Billy)

I'd asked for it.

All of it.

I was hitchhiking so I deserved it. I must have robbed him. I was smoking pot so that meant that I was a bad kid; getting high, robbing, and probably having sex too. She'd thought the worst and the whole ordeal with a man who looked like a school teacher just confirmed it for her. Even my own damn mother believed Ralph.

I was devastated. My soul was completely deflated. So thin that I could hardly breathe. I don't know how I survived the betrayal but I did.

Sometimes I thought of my dad and longed to be with him and talk to him and ask his advice.

If he were alive, everything would have been different. It might not have even happened. Not to me.

So now I had this huge responsibility of getting justice for all the dead girls. And how the fuck was I going to do that? My own mother, my own flesh and blood didn't believe a damn word I said. The cops labeled me as a wild child and wondered who attacked first, me or Ralph? And in the end, the jury believed Ralph.

He was acquitted and set free like he would be many, many times. Over and Over again he would torture, rape, kill and get off to live another day and kill some more.

I was infuriated. I'd nearly died. My friend had nearly died and she has drifted away now, never wanting to breathe a word of this to anyone. Last I heard she was in a mental hospital. She just couldn't handle it.

I could.

I did.

I am.

I'm a survivor and Ralph truly picked up the wrong girl that night. I know he regretted it when I testified against him many times and stared at him in the court room. I never let him see me shudder. He'd never know I was afraid of that rat bastard with the beady eyes. I still remember how dead his eyes looked. It really is true that you can see the soul of a person through their eyes.

His were black as a hundred-year-old oil lying in a pan in the basement of a haunted house. Smooth. Slick. Motionless. Wicked beyond all reason. He was evil incarnate. A demon who straddled me, fighting like hell to kill my light.

I'm still shining, Ralph. You hear me? Can you hear me down there in Hell?

I'm still blazing bright as the full moon on a crisp Halloween night. You can't snuff me out. I'll never die. Even when I'm gone. I'm here. Just like all the girls. They're in the wind, in the beautiful rains that water the flowers in the spring, in the magical snowflakes that fall on my tongue in the cold winters, in the river currents that twirl along, slipping across the bellies of colorful fish, whispering my name, begging me to tell their story.

I hear you, girls.

All of you.

This story is for you.

For all your pain. All your suffering. All you've lost. And I'm so sorry. So sorry a monster robbed you of your breath, stole your right to happiness and sunshine, all the firsts of youth, all the smiles yet to come. I'm sorry God didn't intervene. I hate that He allowed Ralph to be born and you to die. I don't understand it. One day we will.

Ralph was just an extension of Satan. I do believe that. He was Satan on Earth and I fought him. And won. Many, many people never experience an ounce of that kind of evil in their entire lifetimes. I got a hefty dose of it in one night. So much so that I can still taste it.

Bitter. Raw. Spoiled. So remember, girls. I write this in your honor, your memory and your light. And we will one day all dance in heaven. All of us together.

With God.

3 MY EARLY DAYS

I was born late in life for my parents. My mom was in early menopause when she had me at 42-years-old and my dad was 45.

He thought she was having an affair with her hair dresser and just knew I was the new bundle of joy as a result of that affair. He gave her hell about it and really, it was the worst thing my father did to me, accuse my mother of sleeping with another man and having an out of wedlock baby. He was in such turmoil about it, full of so much doubt that even when I was born, my mother was alone. How awful is that?

On January 26, 1958, Chicago was hunkered down as a blizzard blew in, fast and furious. It was my mom's poor luck that she went into labor when he was gone. With my father emotionally and physically shut off from my mother, she was forced to drive herself to the hospital. I was born a blue baby at 4:20 in the morning with the rarest blood in the world, AB-RH-negative. One of my parents was positive and one was negative, so there were a few complications with my blood. However, the biggest complication had nothing to do with blood.

My dad was at a loss for words when I was born. I looked so much like him that he couldn't deny that I was his child. He was instantly smitten and spent the rest of his life making it up to my mother and me.

BABY BETTY LEE WITH SISTER GAIL AND BROTHER
BILLY.

From birth through my teen years, my
mother would compare photos of my father to me.
She thought we looked like twins.

SCHOOL PHOTOS OF BETTY LEE.

He'd been a shit for denying me when my poor mother was pregnant. But like I said, that was the worst thing he ever did to the both of us. He was truly sorry for it and my mother milked those shitty nine months of his rejection for the rest of his life. I was Daddy's girl through and through. My father loved me like crazy. He thought I hung the moon and back then, with my adoring dad at my side, I did. I not only hung the moon, I laid the sparkly stars all across the Milky Way too. I added the rings to Saturn. He made my life and spent the rest of his life loving me like there was no tomorrow.

Summers with my dad were magical. Three

months of sunny perfection. I was spoiled totally rotten. I went to work with my dad and on the weekends, I went to the country club with him to play golf. He let me drive the golf cart, hanging out with him and clients, laughing and having a good time.

That's how amazing my early life was compared to the hell I'd later endure. My parents were upper middle class. I was the baby girl of a very successful man who made his living as Vice President of the advertising agency, Kuttner and Kuttner. His main job was to draw in new business and he was very good at it.

As a very young child, my parents could not keep up with me. And back then, kids just ran wild outside. I was curious about everything, so I'd wander barefoot around the neighborhood. I didn't know a stranger and everyone was friendly to everyone. I'd just walk into a neighbor's home if their door was open. Sometimes I'd go to their backyards to play with their dogs.

I did this all the time. Most of the time my mother assumed I was with my older sister, Gail. Gail assumed I was with my mother so they rarely worried too much. Gail is 12 years older and like a second mother to me so that could be good for days I needed two moms and really, really crappy for days I didn't want two moms breathing down my neck.

One day they were frantic I was gone. For some odd reason, they actually talked to one another that day and realized I wasn't with either of them. I was five houses down in a neighbor's yard. The neighbor lady started taking me door to door, trying to find my parents, asking if anyone had lost a little girl.

My parents and sister were shocked to find out how often I wandered away. This was such a big deal in the neighborhood that there was quite a lot of discussion among the neighbors and my parents about what to do if I should do it again. I was like a caged animal inside. I had to get out and explore and I always found a way out. Unless my parents and sister could monitor me 24 hours a day, I was getting out somehow. I had ways of escaping. There were too many windows and doors and way too many distractions for my family who loved me but trusted me to stay indoors playing.

That just wasn't going to happen. My poor mother and father were about to pull their hair out about this and even my sister was quite upset, at a loss for what to do with me. One brilliant neighbor came up with a great idea.

Why not get Betty Lee some dog tags to wear at all times, just in case she gets lost wandering around? Just like a return to sender stamp on the corner of an envelope except this return to sender would be a return to mommy and daddy stamp around my neck.

So they did. Their little wild child wore a necklace 24-7. I even took baths with it on. It read.
My name is Betty Lee Hanson.
DA8-4448

BETTY LEE AS A YOUNG CHILD.

That was the number to call if someone found me. Crazy, right? It worked. My parents breathed a little easier.

And I got busted. All the time.

My parents' phone rang off the hook.

That didn't kill my explorer heart but my range was now more limited. Mostly I'd go exploring backyards which totally blows my mind today. Who does that? I did. And as a kid. A dog tag wearing kid.

I was like Florence Nightingale for wildlife. I watched the neighborhood cats catch birds, mice and rabbits. My mother and sister were horrified at my nursing skills but I loved working as the neighborhood wildlife ambulance and hospital service. I had an old bird cage I rummaged out of our basement and a shoebox for the mice with paper and rags. I found boxes for the rabbits. Although most of my patients died, either from fright or their wounds, occasionally I'd get to set a bird free to fly another day. I talked to the animals. We had long conversations about the dangers of the wild. I warned them fiercely about the dangers of not only our two felines, Charlie Chan and Ginger, but also the meanest cat in the hood.

Professor.

The old tom cat was a serial killer every single day of his life. He also had a lot of scars on him, so I figured he was the bully of the block. How bizarre to look back on all this now and see that I should have listened to my own lectures to the wildlife and watch out for danger in the wild.

Ralph was my Professor.

Even the comparison made me want to go back in time and find Professor and scold him. He was hunting on everyone's property, without a license and on his own property too. He went nuts, killing every living creature in site. Something Ralph did too.

When I grew tired of that, I started wandering to the very end of our street, at the cross street, Hartrey Street. When I managed to make it that far, there was a whole new wonderland out there as far as you could see.

The Junk Yard.

I was in hog heaven. There was an adventure waiting every day at the back of many factories.

There was the paint factory, a paper mill, a metal stamp place, a coal dump, which was more fun than you can imagine. And there was the car bone yard.

My mother and sister made the mistake of often dressing me in white clothes and tennis shoes.

BETTY LEE ALL DRESSED UP IN HER WHITE DRESS WITH BATON.

The coal pile put an interesting twist on that. A few kids that lived across the street from the factories saw me jumping and sliding down the coal piles and asked if they could play with me. The more the merrier. We made a day out of it, playing in the coal pile. We eventually got thirsty so we went to their house to get a drink of water.

Their mother was mortified when she saw us. They were from Oklahoma and had never gotten so filthy in their little lives. Their mother hosed us down outside and we had a great time laughing ourselves to tears. There was never a dull moment when I hung out with the kids from Oklahoma. Hanging out with me got them grounded a lot though, so it was back to the junk yard for me. There was a skinny place in the fence I could shimmy through and then I'd go look for the junk yard dogs. There were six of them and they lived in the cars.

They were quite vicious but I had my own animal charms and would always persuade them with a frozen roast I stole from the basement freezer. These dogs became my friends and I loved them, visiting them daily, feeding them in the wonderland that was the junk yard. I had a crazy, wild imagination and every day was a new adventure.

So you see, my entire childhood, up to 13 years of age was just about perfect. Freaking Ward and June Cleaver perfect. I never heard my parents fight, not one time and neither did my sister. In my younger years, I went to camp on my pediatrician's ranch in Zion, Arkansas. I learned how to ride horses and spent beautiful summers there.

My doctor was one of the first physicians to treat the mentally challenged with horses. My big brother, Billy was treated at the ranch. He was the victim of a drunken doctor who crushed his brain with forceps during delivery. He had just come from a party when my mother went into labor. Talk about shit luck. My parents noticed problems with Billy at the age of three. He never progressed mentally past five years of age. They were told by doctors to institutionalize him but my dad adamantly refused.

Billy's needs were taken care of at home and the entire family helped out. Our doctor suggested he go to the ranch and the very next year, it was opened for all children so we both went. We were very lucky. I loved to ride. At camp we all had our own horse and learned to care for it. We entered rodeos in town and I won two categories; walk, trot and canter and the barrel 8's, which is how to train cutting and quarterback horses for herding. I never wanted to leave because I was such a great rider and loved horses so much. I even had a cowboy crush when I was 10. His name was Andy and he was 15. He was called a rough neck on the ranch and was a hired hand but God how I was enamored with that boy. Andy introduced me to eating my first snake and you know what? It does taste like chicken.

My fondest memory of riding horses was at a full gallop through a wheat field, with thunder clouds. They make the wheat look silver. Even the thought of it is so beautiful, I think I might cry. My days at the ranch were glorious, sweet days that passed too quickly but oh how they were cherished. The smell of hay and the sound of a horse trotting forms a lump in my throat. I long to ride again. Just take me away to those warm summer days of goodness and peace, where my brother found love and laughter and was a normal kid like me.

Another golden memory I have as a child were the Saturdays my brother and I spent with our dear father. One particular Saturday we were running the usual errands. I was seven years old. We were in our new car, a 65 Chevy, leaving the hardware store and for reasons unknown to me to this day, I threw the biggest temper tantrum of my young life. When we drove I always rode in back and my dad and brother rode up front. Only God knows why I flat out refused to get in the back seat on that particular Saturday afternoon. I lay on the pavement banging my hands into the blacktop of the parking lot. My dad couldn't understand why in the world I was throwing such a huge tantrum but he'd had it so he let me squeeze in between him and my brother. Now my dad was a big man, weighing 245 pounds. He took up most of the seat so it was pretty tight up front but off we go and I stopped throwing a fit.

When my dad made a legal left turn, a drunk driver ran a red light and smashed into our car, making the back window implode into the back seat, shredding it to pieces. When we got out of the car, the police took a statement from my father and he told the officer about my fit, after he had inquired about my hands being cut up a bit. He explained how I refused to get in the back seat. The police officer told my dad that I must be able to see the future and they became lifelong friends. My dad was very superstitious and thought it was very strange that I'd thrown a giant fit and that fit saved my life. He decided from then on that I was psychic. He was the kind of person who believed in signs, good and bad.

On the way to my baptism, the priest had a heart attack so he decided I shouldn't be baptized. I'm not sure if he thought I should be baptized by another priest or what but there was no way in hell I was getting baptized that day because there was a cloud over that particular priest's head. He would flip out if he saw a black cat cross his path or if he spilled salt, he was tossing it over his shoulder. There was no way he'd ever walk under a ladder. He was nuts about superstitions so when I'd thrown that fit, he was convinced that I was special. He paid attention to everything I said or did, wondering what it meant. I was like his little walking, talking crystal ball. He thought of me as a gift and put me up on a pedestal like an angel on Earth. I can't say it was a bad thing but my dad thought I had special powers and had everyone else convinced of this too. After fighting off a serial killer, I think I finally believe him.

My dad truly believed in bad signs too. Warning signs. My sister had a friend named Maria. Maria was over at our house one day and she let me watch Psycho. You know, the horror movie with Norman Bates and the Bates' Motel? My parents came home as we were watching it. I was sitting in the rocking chair during the movie and was so freaked out over a stabbing scene that I flipped backwards in the rocker and broke it and hurt myself. My parents rushed in and my dad yelled at Maria for letting me watch such an awful horror movie. To this day my sister believes my reaction to Psycho was a stern warning of things to come and my father believed it too. He was very disturbed and worried after that incident. And I was totally freaked out. I'd never seen anything so scary in all my life. It gives me chills now to think about it. The warning was clear and real. I remember it vividly. I remember being terrified like the girl in Psycho, being trapped in a confined space with no way out but through the killer. I experienced that terror when I watched it on the screen and then experienced it for real later on in life. It was like a vision of horrors to come and it terrified me for a very long time. To this date I cannot watch that movie.

After my mom put that dog tag around my neck, the whole neighborhood kept a close eye on me. One such person was an artist by the name of Skippy Normile, a dear friend of my mom's. She loved to draw my latest antics. She drew a sketch of me petting the attack dog in the backyard and one of me finding a huge dresser and pulling all the clothes out on the floor. She always drew a halo around the top of my head. She thought I was adorable, though, my mom called me a little hellion. My dad liked the sketches so much he had them put on our Christmas cards every year. That's how crazy my dad was about me. To my mom, I was a little heathen and to my dad, I was the angel on the Christmas card. The Christmas cards led me to a modeling career at Kuttner and Kuttner because my dad showed them off to every living soul. They thought I'd be perfect for this one campaign but I hated sitting still for modeling. I wanted to explore all the different nooks and crannies. I loved the art department and the switchboard operator's desk by the door that led back outside to freedom. I'd watch the operator in awe.

"Kuttner and Kuttner, can I help you?"

She connected them with a thick bungee

looking cord and plugged it into a board that had holes on it, with the person's name beneath. I wanted to connect the calls but I just got to watch in fascination.

I became an international model for my dad's designer client, Vicky Vaughn. I even remember what my line was," Weee, Mommy says I can wear a Vicky Vaughn Petite, Jr.!"

To this day, it blows my sister's mind how much shit I can remember. I can remember the outfit Gail laid out for me, how she did my hair for school pictures, what she was wearing on a particular day to work, like a turquoise skirt with matching sweater and blouse. We spent a lot of time in front of the mirror, putting on her make-up, curling our hair with the pink and blue curlers. Those bobby pins were huge but you had to use the big curlers to get the flip. My sister represented the cool mom. My real mother barely noticed me. I was a nuisance to her.

My mom never really believed in me, not even the day she died. She went to her grave thinking I was a bad kid who got what I deserved, embarrassed of me on her death bed. And that still bugs the shit out of me today. Ralph even stole that from me. No, my mother never adored me like my father did but it didn't help that a monster like Ralph helped to convince her I was nothing because I am something. I was special then and now. And my mother never saw it.

Maybe she did. When I was very, very young. I even took care of her in her final days. I hope she knows that I loved her despite the fact that she never believed in me. I know when she met my dad in heaven that he set her straight. I'm sure it broke her heart and for that, I forgive you, Mom. I know you loved me the best you could and I sure as hell didn't make life easy for you. And my brother, Billy was a challenge too. I felt like the middle child though my brother was older. He was mentally way behind, so I was stuck with middle child syndrome. It was part of my legacy.

Because my dad had refused me in the womb, he showered me with love and affection until the day he died. I forgive you for those nine months you didn't care, Dad. No one's perfect. Not me, not Mom, not you… but we were happy once upon a time and you both brought me into this world. I was a kid you couldn't really stop from exploding all over the place. Even now, I just can't seem to shut up. One day we'll all be together again and it will be like being in that junk yard with those great dogs. We'll play and laugh and hug and talk forever while the sun shines on our faces. We won't have any cares in the world and Billy will be there too. And he'll understand everything. I think he did anyways. And thank you, sis, for being the cool mom I needed. For being the fun mom, for putting up with me all those years when I was a bratty pest. I'm glad you're in my world still.

I love traveling back to those memories. Before the attack. Before I died. Before I went to heaven and saw my Daddy. Those memories are the only bits of my life I care to relive. Once I was in the tunnel I wanted to keep walking. I wanted to sprint toward the light where my father wavered, beckoning me.

4 WHEN I DIED

I regained consciousness in an ER room at Highland Park Hospital. My first memory was of my shirt ripping as nurses cut it off of me. And when I glanced up and out the door, I saw Ralph Andrews smiling at me. I went insane with rage and started yanking my IVs out. A cop materialized and shoved my killer through the door. Nurses screamed to get him away from me. And that was all she wrote. Everything went black again. When I woke up again, my brother was there, screaming, asking if I was okay. I knew he didn't understand what in the hell was going on because he had brain damage. Why in the hell did my mother bring Billy?

My head was swimming in confusion. I went in and out of consciousness and every time my world went black, there was my dead dad. Dead now for six long months. Oh how I wanted to stay with him but he explained that it wasn't my time to go yet. He said I had work to do. What work? My life on earth was pure Hell. I wanted to go to sleep.

Forever.

I wanted an end to this nightmare. Every day seemed to get worse. Why wouldn't he just walk me down the tunnel? I could feel the warmth, like bright white sunrays breaking through the clouds. And when a speck of light hit my cheeks, I was filled with a euphoria and peace there are just no words for, not in any language. And I just know this, though I can only speak English. Some things are just too intense, too real, too good for silly things like words. Those things are reserved for the soul only and my soul wanted more. I was hungry for it. I tried to walk past my father but he was bigger than he was in life and stronger too. He followed me like a shadow. Like an energy ball of fat love that moved with me. He smiled down at me and shook his head and I'd never been so depressed and heart broken in all my days. I knew it wasn't a dream. But it wasn't life as I knew it either. It was something beyond what we humans understand on this rock called planet Earth. This kind of shit doesn't happen down here in Hell. We don't feel these kinds of amazing things while blood runs through our veins.

I'd lost a lot of blood so I guess I got to join the club for a few minutes. Nurses and doctors told me later that I debated back and forth with my father about why I should leave. They said I wept out loud and wailed like a baby throwing a temper tantrum. And I sure as hell felt like one. So close to paradise, forced to go back and suck it up. Face my killer. Deal with life. Deal with my comatose mother, my screaming brother and my sister who was lucky enough to escape her old family life and create a new life for herself.

One thing I can tell you for sure is this. There is a God. And he is Great. I got a tiny glimpse of him. I'm not afraid to die. I welcome it. When my work here Is done, I shall go smiling. And part of my work is writing this book. And because I had that experience, it brings me so much comfort for all the girls.

It isn't fair they had to leave early. They didn't get to live here and get married, have babies, have a career and make love under the stars. None of that is fair but God evened it up real good for Ralph because he created a place called heaven. That's where they are now, basking in all that white angel light. I have a message for those who don't believe.

Wise up. Your time is coming.

Do your best on Earth and be a good person. Help those who need your help. You were born for a reason. For a good reason. Find your purpose and live it. You'll be rewarded for it later.

So basically I had no choice. I didn't want to come back. My father blocked the tunnel and told me I had to go back. He said he'd come for me again when it was truly my time to die. Now I think of death as a new birth, not the end. I welcome my birth when it comes. Don't be sad for me. Shed no tears for me. I will be free. I'll be playing poker with my papa.

5 PISSED OFF

Why didn't they just let me die? I was in paradise. Living in paradise was the happiest memory of my life. Wait. I wasn't alive. I was dead. The happiest memory of my life was my death. How ironic is that?

Even to linger there for one more blissful second would have been sublime. But no. Those nurses and doctors who make their livings doing the work of the angels actually did the opposite that day. They brought me back to Hell.

Back to face my killer. Time and time again I had to testify and see that demon. And to top it off, he had his precious little wife with him at all times. I had to look at her and know this monster had children for God's sake.

Pam and I no longer spoke. Our friendship was ruined. Her saintly father who made money burying my dad only a few months before had decided it was all my fault. He visited me in the hospital. The bastard promised me a fur coat to stay away from his princess. I screamed at him to get out of my room. I was beyond pissed. Back then, anyone who crossed my path would get a hefty dose of my wrath. I was a stone cold, fucking little bitch. I refused to care about anyone or anything and even to this day, part of that stone cold bitch resides in me and rears her ugly head.

Many times while working on this book with Opal, I became that person, for the simple fact that the memories brought all of it back. Going back in time to rehash all this shit, all the murders, all the pain, all the betrayal made me mean at times. Many writers have tried to write this book. It took Opal two years to wade through all the pain, misery, paranoia, angry outbursts, strange bizarre dreams and long phone calls that often had her ready to throw in the towel on this book. Why did she write it? Because she got to know me, despite all my flaws, my accusations, my lack of faith in every living soul alive on this planet. Most importantly, she wrote it because it horrifies her that I nearly died at the hands of a monster and that others did die. Brutal, horrid deaths reserved for fictional horror movies. Ralph led those girls through Hell on Earth. Walked them straight through the fiery gates so they could meet the Devil himself while they were breathing their last breaths.

I met the Devil too. He took me by the hand. I'm no longer pure because of it. I'm like a sea gull dipped in sludge after an oil spill. Only I wasn't rescued and cleaned up by volunteers. There were no volunteers. I licked myself clean. And it tasted like shit. I hated it. I hate it still. This is what you get when someone is faced with Satan himself and lives to tell about it. The bitterness comes to the surface every now and then. I just can't get all my feathers completely white again. I'm now gray. And Opal knows that. She's knows I'm human. Just like her. Just like all of us. All of us except for Ralph. Who knows if he was ever human? Have you ever thought about people like him? Was Hitler a good baby? Was he loved and kissed by his mother? Was he her dream come true? Was Ralph? What happens to people to make them turn so hideous, so against their own kind? I'll never understand it. So don't judge me. I'm not perfect. I'm real. And this is why.

I was a mess. I couldn't really cope with life at all. I walked around with a bodyguard, a friend who was there simply to help me "keep my shit together". He was mostly there to keep me from beating the shit out of anyone who crossed me. At the age of 20, I had a beautiful baby girl, Brandi Lee, but I wasn't ready for a child. I gave her to her grandparents with the condition that they raise her on a farm. I started to come back to life when I got married and had my son, Harley at age 25. My mother adored her new grandson and equally loved my husband, Bill. In a way, this helped to fix things a bit with my mother.

BETTY LEE AND BILL IN HAPPIER TIMES.

HUSBAND BILL, BETTY LEE AND BABY SON, HARLEY.

Remember, she never believed my story about Ralph. She truly believed I brought it all upon myself. Yes, I hitchhiked to a party. But no, I didn't rob Ralph or assault Ralph. I didn't deserve to die at the hands of a serial killer. She had it set in her mind that I deserved my fate. I had it coming. My very own mother thought so damn little of me. Ralph's mother probably rocked him to sleep at night when he was a baby. I was no Ralph. Not even close. I didn't try to murder that monster. He was the killer! He robbed me of what little was left of my childhood. He made my period of mourning over my father even worse. I thought my dad dying was the most terrible thing that could happen to me. How very wrong I was and how much it pained me to know that I was so very alone in the world. It really did make me a bitter person though I tried to go on with life and love my new son and husband.

My happiness was short lived.

After we were married, Bill started drinking a lot and began beating me out of jealousy. I put up with it for 13 long years until we divorced. I was truly miserable. I learned to fight back but one day I'd had enough and was done.

As if I wasn't miserable enough, with each new trial, I became more bitter and angry. I felt such rage at Ralph and the so called "justice system" because every single time they failed to put him behind bars. He continued to assault girls and he continued to get off.

Time after time after time.

I showed up every single time to testify. I felt so guilty because I'd survived and these other girls had not. I wished I was dead most of the time. I dreamed of the girls nightly. I heard them calling out to me. They were proud of me and I knew that but I just wanted to be with them in heaven. I wanted to hug all of them in a big, tight circle and cry for ages. I hear there is no pain and misery in heaven. No crying. How can that be? Do we lose our memories? God, I hope so. I pray we do. That would be heaven in itself. I want to forget.

All of it.

But I can't. If there was an Alzheimer's pill on the market, I would have popped it back when I was 15-years-old. I may have ended up in a nursing home, slobbering on a baby doll, talking about days gone by but I'd be free of the pain and the dark memories of that night and all of those that followed and will haunt me until the day I die.

6 NIGHTMARES

For five to six years after the attack, I had the most violent, horrific dreams you could possibly imagine. In one dream, I was walking down the street when I heard my dogs crying out in agony. Then I heard my mother and brother screaming bloody murder so I ran back to our house and found them all dead. I expected Ralph to be the killer but the killer was this really nice Irish guy that hung out in a local bar with my husband. In my dream I nearly collapsed from exhaustion but I forced myself to keep running. He was after me with a huge machete. It looked like a damn bush whacker and I could see all this blood dripping from it. Suddenly I woke up, breathing hard. I realized I was safe in bed but the pounding of my heart could probably be heard next door.

Later that same day, I went to the bar and was almost killed. Two black men jumped through the glass window and started shooting up the place like crazy. These men underestimated the men in the bar. About eight men started shooting back. The Irish guy, Red shoved me down, out of harm's way. Red was about as nice a guy as there comes but he didn't look it. Ralph did look like the nice guy but was about as horrible as they come. That's all I got out of that dream. Maybe my psyche was trying to teach me not to trust how a person looks. It's what's on the inside that counts.

I had another strange dream. I dreamed I was waiting for a train, one that stops at different points all across town. I got on the train, rode it for a ways and then got off at a library. I go inside and there's a maze of all these stacks and stacks of dusty old books. I can't find my way out. I keep walking faster and faster, then I hear footsteps behind me and they're getting closer and closer. I start running. With each turn, I feel more lost than ever. I wake up confused every single time. Not even sure where I'm at.

Totally disoriented.

i started having that dream after I testified and watched Ralph walk away a free man. I fucking hated him so much. His smug little nerd face. A god damned guy who looked like he would wear a pocket protector and take the teacher an apple every day. I hated myself even more. I couldn't put this fucker away and I'd escaped him. I'd beat his sorry killing ass and still I couldn't help put him behind bars where he belonged. I thought the guilt was going to do me in. When my mother died, she died thinking I deserved to be stabbed by this nice man who had been wrongly attacked by me.

Her own daughter.

I had such hate for him because he'd convinced my mother. And yes, I do realize that I've repeated this several times but it's because I want you, dear reader to know how much it tortured me to experience the loss of my mother's respect and trust.

For a while, friends and family told me they understood how I felt. That only pissed me off more. How the fuck could they understand me? Pretty soon no one wanted to be around me.

Every day that passed, I wished Ralph had killed me. And every Thanksgiving and Christmas, when I thought of all the dead girls, I felt extra shitty and worthless, wishing I would have done a better job on the stand.

But now I'm older. Hell, I've been around for five long decades, plus some. I understand a lot more. The plain and simple truth is that Ralph Raymond Andrews got away with murder for three long decades. Thirty years of torture, rape, stabbing, killing beautiful girls and snuffing out their glorious lights. There are reasons he got away with this. Reasons I will probably never know. But someone knows.

Those three ugly words: Not enough evidence.

I call bullshit. Over and over again. Bullshit, bullshit, bullshit. You be the judge.

Read on.

7 A STRING OF ATTACKS, KIDNAPPINGS AND MURDERS

Ralph left behind an ugly trail of dead girls and one dead man. He was the suspect in a handful of attacks, kidnappings and killings throughout the 70's and 80's. His reign of terror ended in the early 90's when he was finally caught and convicted, after killing 44-year-old Virginia Griffin in 1991.

To this day, I don't understand why this serial killer stayed below the radar, never making national news. All of the data included in this chapter was taken from The Chicago Tribune and can be found on the internet today. But other than the Chicago Tribune reporting the charges, trials, kidnappings, attacks and murders; Andrews was but a blip on the serial killer map. His death in prison in 2006 from a heart condition because he refused to go under the knife was reported as a mere whisper on a few serial killer websites, but his death went mostly unnoticed by the public and the cries of the dead girls only grew more sorrowful, filling my soul with a wounded wailing that just would not die down.

Ralph was only convicted of two killings; his final victim, Virginia Griffin in 1993 and Susan Clarke in 2003, after bragging to a cell mate about raping and killing the 16-year-old girl back in 1977. Officials obtained a confession via a concealed recording device after another inmate informed investigators. Twenty-two years after Clarke's death, her parents were notified of an indictment in the slaying of their youngest child and only daughter. Her parents were distraught at the news, opening an old wound that would never be healed. Ralph had been a suspect in the case as he was for so many others but at the time, there just wasn't enough evidence to charge him with a crime.

Clarke was expected to stop at the home of a child she baby-sat and then later meet up with her boyfriend but never returned home on the night of August 25, 1977. Four days later, her body was found in the weeds of a vegetable garden owned by the Skokie Park District in Illinois. Her hands were bound behind her. She'd been raped, stabbed, eviscerated and shot to death. And to think this went unpunished for 26 years. Until his arrest in 1991 for killing Griffin, the monster was allowed to go to sleep, wake up, go about his day and murder girls for an additional 14 years.

Ralph must have had a thing for killing in gardens because Virginia Griffin was killed in a community garden that both she and Ralph tended together. She was raped and murdered in the same fashion, tortured with a tent pole and a stun gun and of course, eviscerated which was Ralph's signature. In fact, Violent Crimes Detective Larry Thezan working the case recognized Ralph's work and immediately thought of him and all the other girls who were killed in the same fashion, telling his partner that he thought Ralph was the killer. Thezan remembered a letter sent by a retired Skokie detective, warning officers of Ralph who had been a suspect in many cases throughout the northwest suburbs and Michigan. Thezan's partner informed him that Ralph was already being questioned as a witness. Soon it was discovered that Ralph lived in the apartments near the garden.

The murder weapon was found a few hours later in his home. A bloody knife in a bucket of water, as well as a stun gun. Griffin's blood was also found on the inside of Ralph's pants and on a lantern. Ralph was covered in scratches. Griffin had tried to fight back, leaving marks on his face, hands, arms and chest and an arrest was made within a few hours.

In the days to come, the prosecutors answered many calls from detectives expressing years of frustration trying to catch Ralph, believing he was a very active serial killer in the area but never able to prove him guilty time and time again. Why and how did he elude police for so long?

Here's one way he slipped through the cracks. During the death penalty hearing after being convicted for Griffin's murder, a Skokie police sergeant testified that Ralph had admitted to a role in the murder of 15-year-old Amy Alden who was found in 1972 and that of Clarke in 1977. Ralph went on to confess to the sergeant that he'd met Amy Alden in a coffee shop in Evanston, Illinois and said that he did not like to hurt people but he could see his "subconscious" hurting others. He told the sergeant that he imagined seeing the girls' bodies in a garden and a field.

Here's the kicker.

Because this admission was based on

"subconscious recollection", it was not enough evidence to press charges against Ralph. Once again, I call bullshit. What the fuck is that? He admits to killing the girls, tries to wriggle out of the admission by saying maybe he imagined it, so the cops just shrug it off? It would be another nine years before Ralph was even charged with Clarke's murder. Does that make you want to puke your guts out like I do? I thought so. So who is responsible for not pressing charges? The sergeant? The state? How many crazy killers have said wild shit just like that? How does that conversation go?

"Well, I imagined killing them. Not sure though. Oh and I imagine I remember where I dumped the bodies," says the crazy killer.

And the cop says, "Okay. Well, since you imagined the killings, it must not be true. Forget about it."

Yes, this shit really happened. Go Google The Chicago Tribune, COP TESTIFIES THAT KILLER TOLD OF ROLES IN 2 MURDERS by Terry Wilson on July 14, 1994.

Like I said, bullshit.

And that is just ONE of the many times that Ralph got away with murder.

Unbelievable.

Now that's some sloppy police work. Either that or Ralph just happened to be the luckiest killer on the planet. One detective that I know of even turned in his badge after watching Ralph escape justice from what he called an iron-clad case back in March of 1976 in Wyoming, Michigan.

WYOMING MICH
POLICE DEPT
11785 3-10-76
1 9 7 6

Ralph Andrews, after his arrest in Wyoming,
Mich., for allegedly attacking two
women at a gas station. He was acquitted.

Two young women were attacked at a gas
station where Ralph worked at the time. The women
went to relieve themselves in the bathroom. While in
the bathroom, Ralph went under the hood of the car
the women were traveling in and removed the
distributor cap. During the trial, one of the women

testified that Ralph had tied her friend up, threatened her with a screwdriver and raped her. Instead of killing the women, he let them go, after sticking a $20 bill into one of their shirt pockets. Ralph testified that the women had whored themselves out for car repairs. Just like my case, Ralph was acquitted again. The damn jury believed his lies. He was either a fantastic actor or he'd made a deal with Satan. Maybe it was both because time after time he got off, after telling lies to the juries, leaving his victims more raped than before.

Officer Tom Price quit his job when Ralph was acquitted in the gas station rape case. "I knew this man was going to walk out of this courtroom and I knew this man was going to kill someone when he did. That was the end of my career as a police officer," Price told The Chicago Tribune. "I can't protect society from itself, and they didn't protect themselves."

Price turned in his badge after the trial and moved to Florida to work as a computer programmer.

Ralph was a suspect in many cases but again, there was just not enough evidence. The Chicago Tribune listed the dead girls in a huge write-up on December 2, 1994, after he was convicted of killing Virginia Griffin. I'll list them in order of their deaths.

Amy Alden of Evanston, Illinois was 15 when she never arrived at a friend's house to spend the night after a party in 1972. In September of 1972, her skeleton was found in dense brush next to Memorial Park Cemetery in Skokie. Though her belt was found around her neck, her cause of death was listed undetermined and not ruled a murder. (The Chicago Tribune lists Alden's death in 1977 but that date is wrong. This has been verified by her best friend and family friend, Paul Wells and by the actual grave marker at her resting place.)

How the hell does that happen? Her skeleton is found dumped near a cemetery with the belt around her neck and this isn't ruled a murder? Ralph later confessed to his cell mate. He admitted to killing Amy Alden and everyone who knew the case back in the 70's were not surprised because Ralph knew Amy. Ralph drove the city bus where Amy lived. She often took that bus. In fact, the day he abducted Amy, he was in a work release program at the Cook County Jail for another one of his many crimes. The night he kidnapped her, he arrived back at the jail late. Ralph was questioned by police but of course, once again, there just wasn't enough evidence.

According to some of Amy's friends who also rode the city bus, Ralph told Amy in front of many others, publicly on the bus, that he'd strangle her with her own belt if he caught her smoking marijuana. Other kids said that Amy made fun of him and the bus load of kids laughed out loud. (More on Amy's story in a future chapter when we talk with Amy's best friend, Paul Wells who grew up with her and was a friend of the family.)

Robin Feuerriegel, 17, of Evanston, Illinois left her boyfriend's house and disappeared. She was last seen hitchhiking. On November 18, 1972, her decomposed remains were found near the Glenview Naval Air Station, only four blocks from where Amy

Alden's body had been found. Her cause of death was strangulation. Robin Feuerriegel was a friend of Amy Alden according to Paul Wells.

Laura Williams, 16, of the North Side, Illinois was found stabbed to death in May of 1977, only 100 yards from where Robin Feuerriegel's body had been found.

Arvella Louise Thomas, 14, of Chicago, Illinois went missing in April of 1978. She was walking to the train stop late one night when she was without cab fare to get home. She was found the next morning in a Skokie alley, stabbed and strangled to death with her own pantyhose. Ralph was a suspect in this case as well, questioned by police after they found a bloody knife in his car. Ralph told police the blood was deer or fish blood. Back in 1978 we didn't have the forensics we do today but tests did reveal that the blood was not deer or fish blood. Test confirmed the blood was human and was also the same type of blood as that of Arvella Louise Thomas.

Ralph was the suspect in the death of one man in 1982. 51-year-old Floyd Foster was a hunting buddy of Ralph's. Foster's death was ruled a hunting accident, but his son, Jerry Lee Foster who was hunting with the pair, testified at Ralph's sentencing that he believed Ralph shot his father on purpose. This was another big example of Ralph getting off for his crimes and there were witnesses this time. (More on Floyd Foster in a future chapter when we talk with his son, Mark Foster.)

In Ralph's final years in prison, he confessed to kidnapping, butchering and eviscerating as many as 40 girls and women throughout Illinois, Wisconsin and Michigan. Sadly, the families of those killed will never find out and never receive justice.

There were other girls who escaped as I did but not many. A woman who wishes to remain anonymous for this book once dated Ralph in 1978 and agreed to go on a canoe ride in Skokie Lagoon one morning. Remember, Skokie Lagoon is where Ralph told me he would kill me and dump my body, along with my best friend, Pam. This must have been a favorite dumping ground of Ralph's. While the woman was in the canoe, Ralph knocked her unconscious with a whiskey bottle and then tried to strangle her with a scarf. He tied her hands and feet to wooden stakes but miraculously, she escaped. She pressed charges and he was arrested.

Ralph went through another trial but was acquitted of attempted murder charges. He was convicted of unlawful restraint though and sentenced to three years in prison. In February of 1980, he was paroled. My mind was absolutely blown. By 1978, Ralph had a huge record of arrests, former trials and had been the suspect in a handful of murders and once again he got off for attempted murder and received a slap on the wrist.

1978

In Skokie, Andrews was acquitted
of attempted murder charges and convicted
of unlawful restraint.

This sick bastard had the balls to write the woman and her father while he served his time in prison. The letter was quoted in The Chicago Tribune. "Think of my three children. We have had fun and one time I get real drunk and hurt you a little and make a mistake that I am very sorry for...If you let it be known that you forgive me, and you feel that I've paid enough already, then the police will have to let me out of jail."

Pathetic begging from a killer. He's asking his victim to show pity and mercy on him when he tried to strangle her, tied her up and kill her. Hurt you just a little? Ralph scarred that woman for life, just like he scarred me for life. She probably still has nightmares to this day.

Another woman escaped Ralph when he knocked her off her bike and dragged her into his car, kidnapping her. It was 1980, in Michigan. This poor woman was unlucky enough to be his damn neighbor at the time. She fought for her life when he knocked her off her bike. He held a chemical soaked rag over her face and she screamed. Luckily another neighbor heard her cries for help and approached Ralph's car. He was caught but slick once again, deciding to feign the good neighbor and drive her home. The 20-year-old woman ran to her mother while Ralph walked up to her father and told him, "I hit your daughter and I brought her home."

Her mother could smell the fumes from the chemicals he tried to poison her with and confronted Ralph about the scent. Her father demanded an answer, the woman testified in court. His answer was to punch her father. The woman also testified that her mother was distraught when she noticed pieces of rope in the back seat of Ralph's car. The next day, the woman and her mother went to the prosecutor's office to press charges but were told that Ralph had already been in to see him, explaining everything. No charges were filed once again because the authorities believed Ralph's story over the woman's story.

It's important to note that Ralph did have a wife and three kids.

When he divorced, he had a girlfriend for seven long years. So why didn't he kill his girlfriend, Mary Ebeling? We'll never know but she did testify at Ralph's trial when prosecutors were seeking the death penalty for the murder of Virginia Griffin. Her testimony proves that Ralph killed Floyd Foster. Another one that fell through the cracks.

She testified that she was shook up when Ralph returned to their trailer in Ravenna, Michigan from deer hunting in 1982. Ralph told her he had just killed his best friend. She told Cook county Circuit Court Judge Thomas Durkin,

"He didn't seem upset at all-not at all. It wasn't until Floyd's wife appeared that he showed any remorse. He was crying, but it didn't seem like he was really bothered."

She also testified that she was never asked if she knew anything about Foster's death. She added that she had seen Ralph butcher 50 to 75 deer in the seven years she knew him. (Ralph often eviscerated girls and women in the same fashion as a hunter eviscerates a deer.) She told the court of bloodied blankets, a woman's scarf and earrings she found in his Michigan trailer. She asked Ralph about the items, asking whose they were and he told her that they belonged to "the girls". She told the court she assumed he meant daughters of their friends.

All this killing and getting off time after time after time is best summed up by retired Skokie Police Detective Charlie Kitchell who tried to catch Ralph for 20 years. He told The Chicago Tribune that "He got away with a bunch of murders. He was like a carrot in front of a burro's nose-you couldn't get at it."

8 BREAK IN

Ralph hated me more than you can imagine. He wanted a do over.

A do over kill.

I was 19 when he came after me again. The police had warned me and told me they had observed him watching me and following me. These men in blue were good men, men who helped to protect me over and over. I had told my kind neighbors to watch out for him. It was a neighbor who saw him go to my home. He broke the living room window with a crow bar at night. Luckily I was out with friends.

He tried to get inside and attacked my German Shepherd/St. Bernard mix, Dillinger with a crow bar over the head. Also inside were two other dogs, Chako, an albino German Shepherd and King, a full blooded German Shepherd. Who in their right mind would break into a home with three gigantic dogs?

Dillinger bit him and ripped his arm wide open. He fled the house. The cops came and investigated but they had no proof and no one was talking so no charges were filed, though they knew he had tried to break into my home. The cops wanted him behind bars as much as I wanted him dead but proving his crimes had been so tough. They paid him a visit and asked about his torn up arm and warned him to stay away from me. Of course he denied it as he always did and made up some reason why he had the injury.

Ralph always had an excuse and always got away.

9 BERNICE BASS

Over the years, I have come to know many family members of those killed as well as other girls like me who survived this monster. I became very close friends with Virgina Griffin's mother, Bernice Bass. She became my second mother and often told me I was like a daughter to her. We are bonded for life because her daughter died at the hands of that demon.

Bernice was a preacher and worked for the Lord on a daily basis. Her faith carried her through the grief of losing her daughter to a predator like Ralph. She told me that Virginia had lost her way and become a prostitute. Ralph hated women and especially women he considered whores. This was common knowledge to the girls who survived Ralph because of the insults he'd throw their way and the lies he would tell the police about girls exchanging sex for money or car work.

Their punishment for being dirty whores? Death.

Bernice confided in me during the trial. She told me that Virginia had told her that she hit on Ralph. They had shared drinks in the community garden. Virginia was strung out on crack and sold her body for drug money. She was hoping Ralph would pay for her services. There was nothing at this point that Bernice could do but listen to her 44-year-old daughter and stay in touch with her. She was too lost, yet her mother kept in touch and prayed for her daily.

With Virginia's death came justice. Finally. It

breaks my heart to know that another child of God had to lose her life at Ralph's hands. But Virginia would be the last girl slaughtered by the man I fought off in a bloody car nearly twenty years before her death.

Bernice told The Chicago Tribune that she knew her daughter was going to die because she had a very vivid dream. And many of her dreams were premonitions, often warning her of something to come. Sadly, this one came true. She dreamed that Virginia was a baby and she had to cross a great river with her in her arms. As she tried to cross, her baby squirmed and wiggled, making it difficult to get to the other side. After trying three times to cross the river, she came upon a man in black and asked him to take her baby and help them cross. The man took the baby and she was able to cross the river.

When she looked back, the man and her baby were gone. God talked to her. He explained to her that she had carried Virginia as far as she could and that she was going to be killed and would die in Pottawatomie Garden. Bernice even called Virginia and told her the dream to warn her but you know how that goes. Virginia probably dismissed it as only a dream, never expecting to meet her fate in that garden only three days later, dying at the hands of Ralph, burned and shocked over and over by a stun gun, raped and eviscerated with a tent pole, stabbed to death 32 times with her insides spilled into the garden. Bernice's baby girl was found the next morning by a woman walking her dog.

So that's fate? Do you believe in premonitions? I saw the truth in Bernice's eyes when she told me about her dream. She told me as she held my face in her hands with tears in her eyes, "You're the only one that will be the voice for all the dead girls. You talk for the murdered children and victims. Always remember that."

Virginia's final purpose in life was to end the terror that was Ralph Raymond Andrews on this earth once and for all. That's a heroic reason to die. I'm sorry that it happened to her. My heart is broken but her death was the one that put him behind bars for good. Thank you for your sacrifice, Virginia. I know life on Earth was tortuous in the end, even before you met Ralph. I know your life had become a mess. I can only wonder if this was God's way of taking you home, away from the horrors of drug addiction and prostitution.

And in this final hour, when Ralph was caught at the age of 46, he was tired of killing. He didn't try to hide the bloody knife and bucket, the blood on his pants, the stun gun or the lantern with bloody fingerprints on it. He was taken into custody within a few hours and the reign of terror was over. Ralph Raymond Andrews had officially retired from abducting, raping, torturing and killing all mankind.

Andrews after his arrest for the murder
of Virginia Griffin, for which he was sentenced
to life plus 30 years.

Back in the 90's, when I saw Ralph at the trial,
I couldn't believe how much he had deteriorated.
Alcoholism had done him in. He was never a big guy
but now he looked more frail than ever. He walked
and sat all stooped with terrible posture. Most of his
hair was gone and I marveled at the fact that he was
finally..thank you, God..finally behind bars! He had
been a broken, dark, evil soul for years but now it

truly showed. He looked at least twenty years older than his 46. He now looked like the devil I knew him to be. Gone was the conservative, clean cut man who abducted me and convinced many authorities and many juries that he was the victim. The evil within had turned inside out and he looked like a killer to me at that last trial in 1993.

I went to this trial with fierce determination, five days a week. I guess I knew this was my last chance of helping to put him away forever and it weighed heavy on my heart. I knew the evidence was in our favor this time and it motivated me to be strong, to stay focused and to face him for one last trial. I really don't think I could have taken another acquittal. If this monster got away with murder again, I thought I'd lose my ever loving mind. I was still angry, even 20 years later. Two decades had passed since he had abducted me and stabbed me in the heart during that Christmas blizzard and I was not going to give up now. I stared at him every single day. My testimony came during the sentencing part of the trial, in full view of the jury. I had all my ducks in a row. I calculated everything, retelling my story to the very best of my ability. I called the three news stations in Chicago, making sure they aired the news of the trial. I told the media I survived a serial killer and he was now on trial again. I wanted the world to know that I did my best to help put him in a cage.

And how I wished to God I could be the one to lock that cage and throw the key off the edge of the Earth. I like to think I helped. It gave me a small measure of peace to testify and stare at him again. I know he wished to God I was dead. I'm sure he regretted abducting me. I showed up at every trial unless I was ill. I stared at his ugly face more times than I care to remember. I was praying this was the last time I'd have to cast my eyes upon darkest evil. It's a rotten place to gaze. His soul is so diseased. Being in the same room with him was like swimming in the sewer. I just wanted to swim faster and faster to get away but the faster I swam, the darker and more polluted the waters became. There is just no escape from that kind of evil.

It's thicker than molasses, tasting moldy and foreign to my tongue. It always took me time to recover from a trial. It was like having lunch with Lucifer. Like breaking bread with the fallen angel himself. I was relieved. My soul sighed when he was convicted and sentenced to life though I wanted him to receive the death penalty. But really, in the long run, it happened like it was supposed to happen. For some reason, he was forced to live his final days out in prison. The thought of him inside a cage for the rest of his days satisfied me more than I imagined. Not completely though. There are no winners in a case like Ralph's. All those girls had to die and there is no bringing them back.

Ever.

And I wanted to tell my story one day and dedicate it to the girls because they had no voice like I do. They suffered so much. That's the part that really makes me sick. Their suffering keeps me awake at night. I have to remind myself that their suffering is over but it doesn't make it go away. What kind of last thoughts did each of them have? Were they scared out of their minds? Hell yes. Worried their parents would never see them again? Hell yes. But soon, those thoughts drifted away from their tortured minds because the pain was just too unbearable. Each of those girls longed for death in the end, just to have some peace, some freedom from the pain and misery.

While writing this book, Opal had a disturbing dream. She had just interviewed the best friend of Amy Alden, Paul Wells. It was hot summertime. She had been outside speaking to him on the phone but when she hung up and went inside, a chill coursed through her veins. She laid down, feeling like she'd let the heat get the best of her but when she fell asleep, a very vivid, disturbing dream was revealed to her like watching a movie on film.

She saw Amy struggling against Ralph, sitting on the dirt, knowing she would soon die but full of fight. She insulted Ralph. He'd already raped her and was preparing to kill her and rape her again. She spat at him and cursed at her killer and held her head high. Thoughts of her family flitted through her mind. Thoughts of how fucking unfair it was that she was going to die at the hands of a man who had insulted her on the city bus in front of her friends passed through her mind before he came at her again, smiling, wiping blood onto his face, wielding his knife, ready to kill.

She realized she probably wasn't the only one and wondered where the hell was God or his angels when she needed them. She was pissed off. She didn't want to die. She had her whole life to live. This freak of a man was going to steal every bit of that away from her? Why the fuck was he born? Why didn't God exterminate him in his mother's womb? She couldn't believe it but it was true. All this was actually happening. She was living a nightmare and she wanted to wake up and be a girl again. She wanted to see her friends and her mother and brush her long beautiful hair. But he came at her again, stabbing her again. And again and again! She gasped for air! This wasn't fair. She was going to faint. And then she was going to die. Oh God! He just wouldn't stop and he was smiling with her blood all over his face.

The bastard loved it.

This was his only expertise in life. He loved killing and he was good at it. Even when she passed out and her breathing was shallow, she knew. Her soul curled up into a tiny ball and waited. Angels surrounded her. The pain stopped but she could still hear him. He stabbed and stabbed and stabbed. It was over.

She was floating higher and higher. The air smelled clean and so very bright, like the summer scent of hot sunshine on skin. She felt wonderful. She looked down and saw her bloodied body all torn to shreds. She watched as he eviscerated her, then wiped his brow, wiping more blood on his face. He was a monster. Nothing was human about him. She might as well have been attacked by an African lion. She had no chance.

No hope.

But the misery was fading as she climbed higher. He wouldn't win. She was home. No, she wouldn't get to live life as a girl and grow up to marry and make love beneath a full moon and have gorgeous babies. That wasn't to be. But she had a new life now. He killed her life on Earth but she went on and goes on today.

Through all of this, through Opal's dream, and all the horror of the killings, I know one thing. We go on. There is hope. Always. Even in death, there is hope.

10 PAUL WELLS

Amy Alden's best friend growing up was a boy named Paul Wells. Paul was kind enough to be interviewed for this book. Thank you for your input, Paul. I'm so very sorry for the loss of your beautiful friend.

AMY ALDEN AND PAUL WELLS IN HAPPIER TIMES.

Paul commented on a blog I was a guest on called Bonnie's Blog of Crime. He told me that he visited Memorial Park Cemetery to visit Amy's grave. Her body was dumped right outside the same cemetery. Paul's own dad is buried there, along with Amy's mother and grandmother. He visited on Palm Sunday to deliver some palms to the graves. He began chatting with the cemetery groundskeepers while he was there and mentioned Amy.

The groundskeeper responded with, "Oh, that girl ghost."

She went on to tell him that Amy haunts the spot on Old Orchard Road where she was killed. She told him that the detective working on the case sometimes visits the grave and said he'd seen her ghost several times waiting by the road.

That tells me that Amy was not resting as she should. I hope her spirit has gone on by now. I hope Old Orchard Road's only visitors now are creatures of nature; squirrels, birds, butterflies. That poor road will never be the same. There will always be a deep longing and sadness attached to it. I wish I had gone there and seen her and talked to her spirit. Who knows if we'd have been able to communicate or not but I would try to tell her how sorry I was and that I would keep trying until I died to put Ralph behind bars for good.

Here's the email Paul sent Opal before she interviewed him.

September 12, 2012

Amy and I grew up together. We were like Brother and Sister. Our Mothers knew each other in High School, and my Mother was best friends with Amy's Uncle, Bobby who had adopted my Mother's family as his surrogate family, as there were problems in his family. Our Mothers were both widowed as young Mothers in their 20s. My Father and Amy's died of disease early on. Barbara, Amy's Mother and mine instantly became Sisters. Lasted until Barbara died of cancer in 1989. Barbara and Amy moved from South Evanston to North Evanston, to live around the corner from us. Later we moved to another suburb, but saw each other very often and our Mothers spoke on the phone twice a day.

I spoke to Amy on the telephone just minutes before she went out that night. She and her Mother were having a fight about which shoes Amy was going to wear, and it was taking her too long to get going. I knew that Amy had had a dispute with a bus driver, but the way Amy put it, she had emerged the victor by getting the bus full of kids to laugh at him. Amy was wrong. I called the police after she was found and told them about the bus driver. I did not know that they had also been told by others who were there.

Part of me died with Amy. Her death had a permanent effect on me. Not just her death, but how she died. I have never really recovered from it. Even her Mother had spoken to me about it. Barbara was a tough woman and survived it, but not intact. She drank too much anyway, and it got a lot worse and she had to be sent to a dry out facility in Oklahoma. It was never that bad again, but she never stopped drinking. Paul

~*~

When Opal talked to Paul on the phone, he told her Amy had gone to a Labor Day party at 8:30 pm. Amy had a fight with her mother just before she left. Apparently, her mother did not like what she was wearing to the party. Amy went with her friend, Diane. They had bought joints, beer and wine for the party. Amy wanted to stay longer at the party, so Diane left, expecting Amy to show up at her house later to spend the night and go to the first day of school together. Amy never showed up so Diane called her mother, Barbara the next day and told her. Amy was missing for eleven days. Her poor grandmother sat waiting and watching the bus every single day in the pouring rain, hoping she'd get off that bus and go home, thinking she might have run away after the fight with her mother.

AMY ALDEN AS A CHILD.

When Amy's body was found, the police showed up at Barbara's work to tell her the horrible news. Paul was told she let out a terrible shriek. Mind you, Paul had been to the police early on, telling police that he suspected Ralph Andrews all along because he had said on the city bus in front of God and everyone to Amy, "If I catch you smoking marijuana, I will choke you!"

The police did pick up Ralph and interviewed him but released him for lack of evidence. Barbara died of lung cancer in 1989. I can only hope that she was overjoyed when she was reunited with her beautiful daughter. I have faith in that thought. Paul thought it was important to mention that one of Amy's friends, Robin Feuerriegel was also murdered, strangled to death. I mentioned her earlier. She was the girl who was last seen hitchhiking after leaving her boyfriend's house. Her remains were found November 18, 1972, only a couple of months after Amy was killed.

Robin was found only four blocks from where Amy was found.

AMY ALDEN AS A TEEN.

11 MARK FOSTER

Floyd Foster was the only man (to my knowledge) killed by Ralph Raymond Andrews. His son, Mark was interviewed for the book. The stuff Mark shared with Opal creeped her out and even thinking about it now, my blood runs cold. Mark gave us an insider's view into Ralph's life. Mark's father, Floyd and his older brother Jerry were hunting buddies of Ralph's. Mark did meet Ralph and did hang out with him a few times but he was younger and didn't spend as much time with the killer as the other two men.

"Can you describe Ralph for me?" Opal asked Mark over the phone.

"Ralph was about 5 feet, 8 inches; very thin. I'd describe him as ordinary but very creepy. He mostly wore blue jeans and a t-shirt. There was nothing special about him. I have to admit that my wife was comfortable around him. Ralph was a friendly person, very talkative but the first day I met him, the hair on the back of my neck stood up. Mary, his girlfriend was nice but not always around. I know he liked petite women and I was always afraid for my small wife. I knew he wasn't normal. I remember that his mother worked at a place that made candy apples. Ralph was always bringing people those candy apples. He also drank a lot of beer and whisky and he had some type of job in construction or as a contractor," Mark said.

~*~

Floyd Foster's death was ruled a hunting

accident but Jerry (Jerry passed away in 2010) relayed the story to the authorities and said he believed the killing was done on purpose. It was November 21, 1982. Ralph, Jerry and Floyd were crossing a log on a creek while hunting. Jerry had been in Vietnam and Ralph was questioning him about the war.

Ralph asked Jerry, "So, what was it like to kill someone over there?"

Jerry responded. "I don't really want to talk about that."

Ralph said, "I'll show you how we do it here in Michigan."

Then he shot Floyd with a .243 rifle as they were crossing the creek. Floyd fell into the water. Jerry told Mark that his dad's last words were, "Oh my God, Ralph! You shot me!"

And then he was dead, only five days after Mark's son was born. Jerry told Mark that Ralph used hollow points for the very first time when he killed their father. He was bragging about the hollow points.

Ralph lived in a rundown trailer in Ravenna, Michigan. He had no phone so he ran to his closest neighbors, Lois and Clyde. Actually, Floyd was killed on their property. Jerry stayed with his dead father in the creek and waited for the police.

When they arrived, Ralph told them it was an accident. After all, he had run to the neighbors and called for help. Jerry told his version of what happened but it was his word against Ralph's and once again, the police believed Ralph was harmless and ruled the murder an accident.

It makes me fucking sick to know that he so arrogantly asked about Vietnam, then without a second thought, he shot his so called "hunting buddy" to death in front of his son to prove how "folks up in Michigan do it."

Pure evil.

But Floyd wasn't a model citizen either. Mark even admitted to Opal that his father liked the "young ones". He was convicted of statutory rape. I call him a rapist because that's what Floyd was – a convicted rapist.

It was the late 70's when Ralph was sentenced to three years for "unlawful restraint" for tying up the young woman in a canoe and trying to strangle her. Mark was told that Ralph bragged about how he knocked her out with a whiskey bottle and staked her to the ground. Lucky for her, the stakes in the ground were too loose. She was able to escape and swim across the river to freedom.

While Ralph served his time, he met Floyd Foster in prison. He was paroled in 1980 and when Floyd was released, they began hunting together but they didn't just hunt deer. Ralph and Floyd went to middle school and high school sporting events together to watch the kids.

Mark speculated that Ralph had something to do with the disappearance of Deanie Peters from Grand Rapids, Michigan. Today this crime has gone unsolved. 14-year-old Deanie was watching her younger brother's wrestling practice at Forest Hills Middle School with her mother on February 5, 1981. She left to go to the bathroom and was never seen again. *

I'm a believer of signs. The day Opal was
doing research on the Deanie Peters' case, she clicked
onto a page created by the news station, WZZM 13,
still searching for her killer on Facebook. She clicked
onto that page on the morning of September 24,
2013 and this is what she read on Deanie's Facebook
Page. You can go look and verify it for yourself but a
chill shot straight up my spine. I too am inclined to
believe that Ralph had something to do with her
disappearance.

*September 24th is Deanie Peters' birthday. Today,
she would have been 47. One day, she will finally be
at peace. Happy birthday, Deanie.*

Opal copied and pasted the statement above
into this book. For some reason it was highlighted in
black with a white font. She tried to take off the
highlighted print and turn the font to black but it
wouldn't switch over. She tried to delete it and it
wouldn't delete. Both Opal and I wanted this to go to
print as she and I believe that Deanie wanted that
statement read and included in the book, highlighted
in black but unfortunately, Amazon and Barnes and
Noble do not allow that type of highlight in their
books. Opal talked to a formatter about the strange
issue of not being able to take off the black highlight
and white font. He said it could not go to print like
that and she should try again to change it. The very
next day, Opal was able to remove the highlight and
change it to a bolder black font without a problem

though she tried many times to switch it over and then delete it.

This was the second time Opal witnessed someone beyond the grave communicating with a writer by changing the font color. An author friend of hers experienced the same thing when her best friend died. This friend included her deceased friend's name in a new website for her deceased friend's books and the font would ALWAYS show up as a white font, no matter how many times she changed it back to black. The font is still white to this day.

Deanie is only four years older than Opal. She can't help but mourn for this girl who was never allowed to live. Opal has contacted WZZM 13's Deanie Peters' Facebook page and shared with them what Mark told her about his speculations of Deanie's disappearance. She encouraged the news team to obtain the cold case recordings of Ralph Andrews if possible. Opal was told the tapes have been destroyed when she called the prison. Ralph admitted to killing 40 girls on these tapes.

Mark remembers that Ralph often gave venison to his family. And when Ralph delivered the deer meat, he always said this, "My sausage has a special ingredient."

Mark wonders now what in the hell was in that sausage. He also remembers something really creepy that happened a few days after his father died. The police had brought his father's clothes over in a paper sack. The sack was sitting by the front door. Ralph came over to deliver some venison. Mark said that everyone else left the room to go to the kitchen or other rooms, leaving Ralph alone in the living room for a few moments. When they returned to the living room, Ralph was gone but his father's clothes had been removed from the paper sack and laid out on the sofa as if his father were lying there; his shirt lying where his chest would lay, his pants lying where his legs would lay and his shoes at his feet. Mark has no proof of who did this with his father's clothes but they suspected it was Ralph because who in the hell else would have done a horrible thing like that?

Mark said that Ralph had often been caught poaching deer and had even served ten days in jail for it. He said he does remember that the police came out to Ralph's property with x-ray machines (Mark's words) but found nothing. He said the police suspected that Floyd might have run across Ralph's "killing fields" and was killed for it. Mark and Jerry both believe that their father knew something about all the girls killed and because of that, he died. Ralph's septic tank was also searched. Opal asked Mark if he remembered a wood chipper on the property. He said there was not a wood chipper on the land. It is also important to mention that Mark said Ralph's property, bought for him by his mother, went on for acres and acres. Possibly up to ten acres. He doesn't believe the police searched the property thoroughly enough.

Mark showed Opal exactly where Ralph's property was on the United States Google Satellite Maps online and what struck her most was the enormous amount of woods behind Ralph's home. It went for miles and miles and is still a wooded area today. Someone else owns Ralph's property now. I wonder if they know what lies beyond their home. I believe the girls are buried there. It is possible he dumped the bodies in and around Chicago like he did the girls killed in the 70's but my gut tells me that they are still on that land today. Even though the police did search the land, I don't believe they searched it thoroughly enough or went deep enough into those woods with their equipment. It would have taken weeks or possibly months to search all the acres that extended beyond Ralph's home. It is important to note that he also frequented the land owned by his neighbors, Lois and Clyde with total freedom. So now we're talking about two gigantic areas of land where Ralph could hide the bodies. Acres and acres and miles and miles of wooded dumping grounds.

Just before this book went to print, Mark emailed
Opal with something else he'd remembered. There
was a tall tree about 40 feet from Ralph's trailer with
a 12 to 14 foot ladder laid up against it. At the top of
that tree was some kind of hole, like a squirrel would
live in. Mark always wondered why the ladder was
there, leading up to that hole. Was that a place for
Ralph to hide his trophies of the girls? Did he hide
rings, necklaces, earrings, panties, photos, or other
things belonging to the girls? Serial killers love their
trophies. I wouldn't doubt there are still some items
up inside that lonely old tree. Sentimental things that
once belonged to beautiful girls. All who are dead.
Some are still missing, never to be heard from again.

*(More disturbing is that when Mark told
Opal of this, he said that Deanie was missing from
Ada, Michigan. The road the school was on is Ada
Drive. The city is Grand Rapids. The fact that his
memory had forgotten the exact name of the town
and replaced it with the road name is pretty eerie
though there is a suburb in Michigan also named Ada.
Had his father told him something all those years
ago?)

12 JOHN PYSKATY

John Pyskaty was a skiing and hunting buddy of Ralph's and the most thorough, helpful person who was interviewed for this book. Opal gleaned more information from John than from anyone else and received some valuable inside information. She was able to get a real glimpse of the life of Ralph Andrews through the eyes of a friend. Thank you, John for your interview.

John met Ralph at the Lake Shore Ski Club in the early 80's, from 1982 through 1984. He provided a few photos of Ralph in the ski club. These photos are invaluable and again, a fantastic glimpse of the monster in action.

John said that when he met Ralph he was working as an electrician and remembers as time went on that Ralph seemed to be getting more and more dangerous, refusing to put away guns while drinking and that was why their friendship broke up and John decided to stay away. Good decision, John, it may have saved your life in the end. Floyd Foster didn't have the foresight to see it that way, maybe because he was a convicted felon himself.

It's also important to point out that John remembers spending the night in Ralph's trailer while deer hunting. He was pretending to sleep when Ralph crossed the room and stole money out of his wallet. John never mentioned this to Ralph, thinking he must have really needed the money but this reassured him that Ralph was a thief just as he had been when joining another man in a Hawaiian business venture and then selling all the equipment to keep the money for himself.

These were the kinds of stories Ralph told John so he knew he was a thief and a liar but never thought he was a killer.

When he found out years later, it frightened him to know how close he may have come to certain death. Luckily for John, Ralph didn't view him as a threat, though John was on his property many, many times. John told Opal of all the bones he saw scattered about the property. He asked Ralph about them and Ralph always said the bones were those of deer. He even mentioned what Ralph told him was a dead skinned deer hanging, but John wasn't sure it was a deer. He really couldn't tell what in the hell it was, just hanging there with the meat exposed and no skin.

He emailed Opal very detailed emails about Ralph.

~*~

June 8, 2013

Hi,

I knew Ralph from the late 70's through the middle of 84. I used to lead AYH, Sierra Club, and Lake Shore Ski Club trips. I was out to his place in Michigan about a dozen times. Take a while to write down all I remember about him. One of the things that really troubled me was how he talked about "accidentally" shooting and killing his best friend Floyd, not with remorse, but almost excitement. He became joyous boasting about how the police returned his .243 bolt action rifle to him. Having learned of his serial killing I very much doubt that the killing was accidental.(He claimed that they were walking across a fallen tree that spanned a creek on his property. Floyd lost his balance and Ralph pushed the muzzle of his rifle out to him, which he grabbed, and when he pulled on it for support Ralph accidentally touched the trigger and it went off.)

Ralph used the clubs to pick up women. (Ironically one time he was the driver of a RV Lake Shore Ski Club rented to go to the Birkebinder race in Wisconsin, he had boasted of having driven a bus.) Having learned that he was a killer I wonder how many he murdered. He liked to boast about his trailer out in the north woods and tried to talk women into going with him up there to enjoy the outdoors without having to camp. I would agree with you that the Chicago police did not want to search his place because it would have shown just how much their failure let him get away with. There were bones all over the place - supposedly deer he had got.

He preferred to poach over hunting or fishing legally. I always thought that was stupid, I preferred to stay within the law. He was always getting caught and spending more money on fines than if he had stayed within the law.

But in retrospect, I guess it was not about hunting or fishing but about breaking the law that was the point of the exercise for him.

He kept sinking further and further into alcoholism and I was becoming afraid to be around him and firearms. I finally gave him an ultimatum, that he stopped drinking when we were hunting or I would not go to his place anymore. (I would give him money for gas, food, etc., when I came up.) His response was, "You can stop drinking around guns, but I'm not, it's not a problem." So that was it. (The incident that had caused my request was his having thrown a loaded pistol, safety off, to one of his friends in Michigan. The guy caught it without it going off, but it terrified him and me while Ralph just laughed and laughed, obliviously to how dangerous that was.)

I don't know if you want me to write all the experiences I remember about him and his place. It would take a few pages and a little while to remember. I think I even have a picture of him with the Lake Shore Ski Club Birke trip somewhere. I went back to school and got my masters in psychology after having gotten injured in a trip up to Ralph's place in '84.

Sincerely,

John Pyskaty

LAKE SHORE SKI CLUB. RALPH ANDREWS AND
JOHN PYSKATY. (Ralph is in the center, white sweater
with a white hat on, his arms around two women.
John is crouched down in the front.)

LAKE SHORE SKI CLUB. (Ralph is 3rd from the right
with his arms around the two women.)

June 10, 2013

Ralph is third from the right in the picture of the racers, he has sun glasses on, a lake shore ski club knit hat, and his arm around the gals on either side. I am in the picture of the entire group, crouched down in front, wearing a lake shore ski club knit cap, glasses, and a small camera in my hands.

The picture flatters Ralph. He had already gone way downhill and been kicked out of AYH and Sierra Club by that point. On a Sierra Club camping trip, he got extremely drunk in front of the campfire and pulled a gun out and announced to the leader "You don't have to worry if a bear comes around tonight, I can take care of him". (I heard this second hand, but knowing Ralph, it was totally consistent with his character.)

I'll talk with you tomorrow.

Best regards,

John

~*~

Opal responded to John's emails and sent him The Chicago Tribune's newspaper article from December 2, 1994, written when Ralph was convicted of killing Virginia Griffin, detailing all his crimes. Here is his response.

June 11, 2013

Opal,

The article sure echoes everyone's feeling
toward Ralph and murder, "I have no trouble
imagining him doing it". Even though you feel that
way around a person, the fact that they are out in
society makes you think you must be wrong, and you
feel guilty and embarrassed. Your mind goes to
thinking that this is a stereotype you are responding
to, perhaps from watching something like
"Deliverance" where hill people are shown as
murdering psychopaths. Sometimes stereotypes are
correct though.

I remembered something about the knife.
Something that was tugging at my memory. It was
not Mike Hammer, but Matt Helm that used a Buck
Lock Blade folder. From the Smith and Wesson
Forum "To this day I carry I carry a Buck knife because
of Matt Helm." This was a series by Donald Hamilton.
The following is a synopsis of the first book in it from
Wikipedia:

Death of a Citizen is a 1960 spy novel
by Donald Hamilton, and was the first in a long-
running series of books featuring the adventures
of assassin, Matt Helm. The title refers to the
metaphorical death of peaceful citizen and family
man Matt Helm and the rebirth of the deadly and
relentless assassin of World War II.

The book sees Matthew Helm, a one-time

assassin and special agent for the American government during the war, being reactivated (code name: Eric) when a former colleague turns rogue and eventually kidnaps Helm's daughter. Afterwards, he agrees to return to duty as an assassin and counter-agent working for a secret agency run by "Mac," his superior officer from 13 years earlier (although published in 1960, the story itself takes place in 1958).

Death of a Citizen is notable for its grimness of tone and events as compared to the usual thriller of the late 1950s and early 1960s. After a few initial missteps as his "citizen" persona is shucked off, Helm re-becomes the competent, hard-boiled, and ruthless agent he had been earlier. The ending of the book is particularly shocking, perhaps, in that he shoots down an adversary who is not directly threatening him and then tortures and kills the person responsible for kidnapping his baby daughter. As a result of his actions, his daughter is rescued — but as the book ends his peace-loving wife is staring in horror at the bloody-handed monster that her apparently sedentary husband has become.

Hamilton would write a total of 27 Matt Helm novels between 1960 and 1993 (with a 28th volume as yet unpublished). The books maintain a loose continuity between each other, although later volumes would downplay Helm's Second World War connections in order to keep the character up-to-date. In the late 1960s, several motion pictures starring Dean Martin as Helm were produced; these films were produced as comedies and contained little of Hamilton's concepts.

I think this is pretty chilling when we talk about someone that the law looks the other way on. That the knife they carried was the same as that carried by a fictional U. S. Government assassin.

Be careful.

From the internet, a picture of a Buck Folding Lockblade. The type Ralph had, and the type used by the fictional government assassin Malt Helm. ~ John

~*~

I'm not sure why John warned Opal to be careful. After all, Ralph has been dead for seven years. What does she have to fear? The warning did make both of us a little too uncomfortable though. He wrote her again eight days later.

June 19, 2013

Hi Opal,

Sure would appreciate if you could add a caveat that like the other people and even the clubs, none of his behaviors were that suspicious to us. Even when we severed relationships with him, it was because we thought his alcoholism had made him dangerous to himself and those around him, not that he was a killer. (The Sierra Club trip leader that blacklisted him for bringing a gun on a trip could have called the police on him for having a concealed gun, but didn't.) There was no way to know he was a murderer. He was just an electrician that drank too much (not unusual for the construction trade), almost a hill person, was looking for companionship, and had a trailer up in the woods.

It is only after you know that he was a killer his actions take on completely different meanings. (It is not like he presented with a swastika tattooed on his forehead. You have the picture of him with Lake Shore Ski Club. If you had been on the trip, you would see that he was lower social economic class compared to the others, but that is nothing.)

I think it was the first time I went up to his place he took me to a little stream where salmon spawn. It was about twelve feet wide and very shallow. Sure enough, we see a huge one, back sticking out of the water coming upstream. He says he is going to make a spear from a broken branch and get it. He takes out his buck knife and sharpens a point on the branch. He tells me to stay down stream and chase it back up to him if he misses.

Well, I don't want to get wet and no one is around, so I take off my clothes and shoes and put them on the bank and get in the shallow water. Of course Ralph strikes at it and does not get it. It heads down towards me and I chase it and it goes head first into some tree roots and I jump on it getting my hands in its gills while being very careful of its dorsal spines since I am nude. Ralph joins me and we lift the salmon out and take it back to clean. I always loved telling that story because it was the biggest fish I ever caught and I did it bare handed and bare. Not anymore.

Now looking back I don't know if Ralph was even trying to catch the fish. He may have only been trying to stab it and leave it to suffer, and my catching it was an accident he had not anticipated nor wanted. My being there might have only been to be able to perform his lie to an audience.

You keep thinking with him it was all about hiding out in plain sight.

I told you about the guy he was supposed to go with to Hawaii with, but Ralph sold their gear. After talking with you I wonder if the guy actually made it to Hawaii. Maybe Ralph just killed him and sold the stuff. Ralph never told me his name.

If you get permission to go to the site of his trailer, it would be interesting if you could bring along a metal detector and backhoe. Probably an anthropologist would be a good idea too, since without knowing it is hard to identify bones.

I have a friend that went up there hunting with me one time. I think it might have been the time I got the fine from the game warden on. Do you want me to see if he is willing to talk to you about Ralph?

Have not had a chance to get that last ski club picture developed. Not that many places do black and white negatives. It is in the van, next time I am in Monterey I will drop it off.

Best regards,

John

~*~

Opal wrote John back and told him that yes, she'd like to talk to his friend. She also mentioned Lois and Clyde to him as the couple who lived on the land next to Ralph's ten acres, identified by Mark Foster. John had seen a large woman stab a pig and Mark told Opal of their little girl who was run over by a car. Here is his response.

June 25, 2013

Hi Opal,

Talked to my friend, he does not want to be interviewed about Ralph. First he said Ralph might come and get him if he got out - he did not know Ralph had died. He is very conservative. He only went up there one weekend with me and felt he did not have much he recalled, other than it was believable that Ralph was a killer. Like everyone, he did not suspect, but after hearing, did not doubt. He said he would buy the book when it is published.

You are right that it was Clyde and Lois. I think Clyde was also the guy Ralph threw the loaded pistol across the room to. The story about a little girl being run over rings a bell, too.

I am very surprised to hear that Mark Foster (Author note: Written in error-it was Jerry Foster who witnessed the shooting) saw the shooting. I believe that was before I knew Ralph. I had only heard Ralph's story, and in that, he and Floyd were alone crossing a fallen tree spanning a creek. He never said anything about Floyd having a son.

Still would be interesting to go up there with a backhoe and metal detectors. Ralph lived there a long time after the Foster shooting, and if the place had been searched, he might have felt it was safe from further inspection. I thought one of the jail house stories on the internet about him indicates that he boasted he buried them on his property in Michigan.

There is one more question, of course. Did the police really want to find anything? Even out there they are politically motivated, and serial killers are not good for tourism or showing themselves as being in-adept by having not caught him sooner. Betty's thesis that the FBI or some government agency had an interest in his work being over-looked comes into play. Remember my joke - do they want to find Jimmy Hoffa's body?

By the way, for a while Ralph had a horse. He bought it at Ravina* (Author note: actual spelling is Ravenna) where they would have a market and auction of livestock. Poor thing was always half starved. I don't remember him ever riding it. What sticks in my mind was how spooked it was one night by Ralph cleaning a deer in the barn that the horse was kept. The skinned deer hanging from the rafters looked almost like a person.

One more thing that has a different meaning when it is known Ralph was a killer. Even though Ralph didn't care enough for the horse to keep it fed, many women are enamored of horses. I can imagine him enticing someone with talk of his place in the woods where he even had a horse. Now his having it makes sense. It was bait for his prey.

Best regards,

John

(A Post Script added by John) Ralph used to tell a story of how he bid on a lot of chickens without having knowing how many were involved. He ended up buying something like 100 live chickens at 25 cents each. Said he did a lot of cleaning and freezing of poultry that weekend. Again, knowing his secret, maybe it was on purpose that he put himself in the position of having an excuse to slaughter 100 animals. Always that other side that was lurking out of sight.

~*~

I spoke with John myself over the phone over the summer. Here's his email to Opal about that conversation.

July 3, 2013

Hi Opal,

Betty Lee wrote me and wanted to talk and we did so about a week ago. I found it quite startling. I really want to think it through a little longer to better articulate my thoughts about what she told me. I had only known about Ralph's getting away the first time, and a version of the Floyd shooting that was far different than what she related. It is incomprehensible that he cold bloodily shot him in front of his son and got away with it.

There is an old joke. When you walk down the street and don't see anyone, you have just seen a secret agent.

It seems there are too many escapes here to chalk up to luck and in-adeptness of police and the courts.

On the other hand, we know our country has

enemies within its borders that need eliminating the agencies constrained. Look at how people fret over the treatment of terrorists even after 9/11. Using actual agents or paying assassins leave a trail that would lead back to someone.

A "get out of jail" card would not. The only people able to expose it would be the assassin and the handler, neither of whom is likely to.

Because of that, it is safe for you and I to speculate about it. Otherwise I would not be writing this.

Betty may have really not just escaped, but finished off Ralph. Her hounding him got him to talk about his murders. If there was a get out of jail card and he started to eventually talk about it, isn't a heart attack convenient?

We may recoil in disgust at the thought that the government would look the other way while someone murdered 40 or more women, but one bomber can take out that many. There is no such thing as a free lunch. I cannot imagine how the people in charge handle dealing with choice of leaving a terrorist out there that has not done anything but they know will. I assume they choose the good of the many over the few. Perhaps a horrible price is being paid* because of those that worry more about the rights of terrorists than averting victims.

Ralph was very good at making bodies

disappear. Again, it is like the secret agent joke. It is just a thesis to explain his fantastic luck, totally no way to prove, and in being so is its beauty.

A different part of the story of Ralph. Going through my old American Youth Hostels papers, I found one with listings of planned canoe trips for 1985. Looks like Ralph lead a whitewater trip for them 9/20/85. I have not been able to find a copy that has the trip announcement in it. I will keep looking. You might want to contact them and see if they can copy the complete trip announcement from an issue that has it.

I vaguely remembered he had been on my whitewater trips and he may have started leading some. I trained a lot of the people who went on to lead trips. (I vaguely remember having a photo of him in whitewater, I have to keep looking. I moved out here three months ago and my photos were never organized.)

Best regards,

John

*As we discussed, there are a lot of serial killers out there not being caught.

~*~

As John mentions, I did hound Ralph for years and years. I mailed him in prison by contacting his cell mate, Kenny Scheiff. This was the only way he would communicate to me. A dumb mistake on my part, I sent the originals to a CNN reporter who was originally going to write the book. The reporter was unable to finish it and never sent the letters back. I have no copies of them. I have asked him many times to send them to me or to Opal. Opal emailed him three times. He assured her that he would scan the letters and send them as soon as his work let up. A few weeks passed and she received nothing so she emailed him again, gently reminding him that we really needed those letters.

He wrote her back saying that he went through several boxes and just doesn't have the time to go through the huge amount of boxes that contain all the research for the book. He couldn't find the letters and was too busy.

This was pretty upsetting to both Opal and I but what can we do? So this book goes to print without those valuable letters. I trusted this CNN reporter with my property and now I have nothing to show for it. Lesson learned.

If he ever has the time to search through the boxes, finds the letters and sends them, then the letters will be added to this book.

So, as a note and a special plea, if the CNN reporter would like to send the letters, we would welcome that addition to the book. Opal and I both understand that he is a busy man and respect his time and commitment to CNN.

~*~

John wrote Opal one final time.

July 23, 2013

Hi Opal,

I finally found a Walgreen's that would do a black and white enlargement. It is a pretty good picture. That's why it was missing from the rest. I must have given the original to Ralph. He totally looks like a normal member of Lake Shore Ski Club, with the exception of the glasses hiding his eyes that you had pointed out.

I was a little surprised that Betty said after talking with me she had slept a full eight hours for the first time in years. It makes sense though, people need to have theories that give structure and meaning to the narrative that are their lives. Just always seeming to be on the wrong side of chance does not. She certainly has had a rough go of it.

Best regards,

John

I still have to search the rest of the pictures. You slow down when you get on the wrong side of 60.

LAKE SHORE SKI CLUB. (Ralph in the center.)

Opal contacted the Lake Shore Ski Club and it is still in existence today with many members who have been in the club for decades. No one had any additional information to add to the book or perhaps they just didn't want to come forward with it.

13 GAIL HANSON KENT

Gail is my 67-year-old sister. She is older than I am. And because she was there watching all this horror unfold and knows me better than most, she was interviewed for the book. To let you know how close knit of a community we were in Evanston, Illinois, read on.

Gail told Opal that her husband's brother, Danny was a good friend of Ralph Andrews. Also, Ralph dated a good friend of Gail's for three years. Her name is Lee Ann Cohen. Lee Ann Cohen's name to this day makes me screech in agony. She was the girl who testified against me in the trial, telling the jury what a wonderful young man Ralph was to her and that he'd never hurt a soul. She went on to defame my character. The jury believed her and Ralph.

I was charged instead. To this day, my record was never expunged. And my mother went to her grave thinking I tried to rob and kill Ralph Raymond Andrews, a nice city bus driver. Thanks, Lee Ann. What a gem you are to society. There were others who believed my story and one of them was my sister.

Gail told Opal that she was extremely upset at my abduction and near murder but felt helpless because there was absolutely nothing she could do about it. She was just horrified because as she told Opal, I'm her very best friend in the world. She described me as having a heart of gold and a very good person. I lived with Gail in Kansas for a while when our dad got cancer when I was in 7th grade. She told Opal we both had a beautiful childhood and I totally agree. She said she can pick up the phone and call me, grounding us both, making our day. And that's true. She is my rock and I am hers. We are bonded like glue for life.

She sent this email to Opal after their talk.

~*~

August 23, 2013

Hi. Here is a little more info for you.

My ex-husband traveled a lot when we lived in Kansas.

A lot of Betty's friends came over to our house when he was gone. We made pizza, brownies and played a lot of canasta. We went swimming after hours and one time Betty's shorts got caught on the fence and I had to pull her off. We had a lot of really good times.

My ex-husband was physically and verbally abusive when he wanted to be. One day Betty walked in the house from school and saw him hitting me and she jumped on him and punched him in the head and said "Why don't you fight somebody that will fight you back." From then on he hit Betty a lot. I guess I went into shock and just froze.

Because of this, Betty and I think this is why she was able to fight off the serial killer. When a friend of mine from work baby sat for Betty - one time she let Betty watch the movie "Psycho". A thought came to my head sometime in the last year or two that maybe the fact that Betty watched that movie was a warning of things that might happen to her in the future.

Because of all the horrible things that happened to Betty and I, no matter how much we argue or disagree, we will always love each other and not only be sisters, but best friends.

To show you the trust we have in each other, I sent my two sons (at different times) to Betty's for her to take care of in the last several years because they were having problems.

Hope this helps. ~ Gail

HAPPY DAYS WITH BIG SIS, GAIL. (Gail on the left,
Betty Lee on the right.)

14 MY FINAL THOUGHTS

It still boggles my mind to find out that the system is so corrupt that this monster had a number of trials and only served time for lesser chargers until his eventual capture in 1991. At Virginia Griffin's trial in 1993, I went five days a week and sat so I could stare right at him. He was not going to get away with it this time, by God! I called the three main news stations in Chicago. I told them that I was a survivor of a serial killer by the name of Ralph Raymond Andrews.

On my front lawn I gave interview after interview to every TV station that came out, as well as The Chicago Tribune. I did all of that because I knew as soon as the District Attorney's office tried to find me, they would not let me say one word to the public and again he might walk. I could not let that happen ever again. Over my dead body would that poor excuse for a human being ever touch one more girl.

Ever.

No more PRETTY LITTLE GIRLS for him to slash to pieces, rape before, during and after he killed them. No way, no how!

Once again, Lee Ann Cohen testified as she did in my 1974 trial. She told the jury that I was wild, crazy and she would not put murder or armed robbery past me. I believe she was still in love with Ralph. So ridiculously in love with this monster that even two decades later, in 1993, she went to the Griffin trial and sat right next to me, hoping to make an ass out of me again. But, the only problem with that was I had reality in my corner. I was ready for Ralphie's favorite girl. I knew it would prove to be a very interesting day and I was not disappointed.

As they described in great detail the charges against him, a picture came up on a screen for all to see; the girls, their deaths, how he did it and for how long he had been doing it. As I watched her turn blue and ashen, the two of them staring at each other, then at me, I had my very first victory against Ralph. Back in 1974, they told the world that a 15-year-old girl was a would-be murderess and thief.

The jury bought their story. And so did my mother. Back then I didn't have my own lawyer. My dad was dead and my sister's good friend was whispering into my own mother's ear that Ralph was a sweet country boy. The trial was already a done deal. Ralph and the state had a perfect witness. I had NOTHING.

When it was all said and done, two Highland Park, Illinois detectives came to my home and told my mom that he was a serial killer and that they were quitting the force over what he had gotten away with because it just ruined their faith in humanity.

So when I faced Ralph again in 1993, I wanted to rip his throat out with my own teeth. I had that much hatred for the man I call a cold blooded rapist and killer. I had suffered a lifetime of pain because of him and his girlfriend who testified against me, giving him the green light to go back out into the world to kill again and again and again.

Rest in peace, Mom, you didn't know. I don't

blame you.

But Lee Ann knew. Now she was going to hear it all. I savored that day for a very long time. I still smile about the look on their faces. For me, that was a triumph for GOOD, a victory for all the girls.

Ralph received life in prison, not the death penalty that the prosecutors promised me. I was severely disappointed but grateful he was put away. It was then that I vowed to torture him through letters, reminding him as often as possible that I was still out there, surviving every day and would one day tell the story. The policemen on the case became my friends. They checked in on me through the years and I visited them. To all of those brave, caring men, thank you.

And to *you* dear reader, thank you for listening.

I am a survivor.

This book is dedicated to all the girls.

Until we meet in heaven.

God keep you.

Wait for me.

ABOUT THE AUTHOR

Opal Roux lives in the Deep South with her husband and three beautiful children. She writes romantic paranormal and vintage novels under the pen name, Alisha Paige. Her cowboy romances and romantic thrillers are written under the pen name, Ruby Vines. You can find her children's books under the pen name, Wolfgang Pie. This is her first True Crime novel.

She loves dark chocolate, red wine, autumn nights and her kitty cat curled at her feet. Her favorite books to read are historical novels and biographies.

You can visit her at her websites at www.Alishapaige.com and www.wolfgangpie.com.

Other Books by this Author

Alisha Paige Books
Canyon Wolf Bride (Paranormal Werewolf Romance)
The Wooden Nickel (Vintage WWII Romance)
Nocturnally Vexed (Paranormal Shapeshifter
Romance)
Voodoo Moon (Paranormal Werewolf Romance)
The Hour Glass Witch (Paranormal Time-Travel
Romance)
Circle City: Lord of the Wolfen ~ Book I (Paranormal
Werewolf Romance)
Uncaged (Paranormal Shapeshifter Romance)
Paranormal 5-Book Collection (The Very Best of Alisha
Paige's Dark, Sensual Romance)
Love Legends (Romance Collection)

Ruby Vines Books
My Little Texas Tornado (Cowboy Romance)
Deadly R&R (Romantic Thriller)

Wolfgang Pie Books
Tusk (Ice Age Adventure for Boys and Girls)
Hunting for Fireflies (Fantasy Adventure for Boys and
Girls)

SOURCES

Website: Bonnie's Blog of Crime
http://mylifeofcrime.wordpress.com/2006/12/06/ser
ial-killer-ralph-raymond-andrews/

Scharnberg, Kirsten (October 13, 2001). "'91 Slaying Evidence Will Be Tested for Use in 2nd Trial." Chicago Tribune, web p. 1.

Wilson, Terry (July 14, 1994). "Cop Testifies That Killer Told of Roles In 2 Murders". Chicago Tribune, web p. 1.

Wilson, Terry (December 2, 1994). "Serial Suspect". Chicago Tribune, p. 1-2.

Wilson, Terry; Hill, James; Cox, Brian (May 26, 1999). "Inmate Is Charged in Girl's '77 Slaying". Chicago Tribune, web p. 1.

48448563R00074

Made in the USA
Lexington, KY
30 December 2015